Wright Family

Census Records, Deed Records, Land Tax Lists, Death Records and Probate Records
Appomattox County
Virginia

Robert N. Grant

HERITAGE BOOKS
2006

HERITAGE BOOKS
AN IMPRINT OF HERITAGE BOOKS, INC.

Books, CDs, and more—Worldwide

For our listing of thousands of titles see our website
at
www.HeritageBooks.com

Published 2006 by
HERITAGE BOOKS, INC.
Publishing Division
65 East Main Street
Westminster, Maryland 21157-5026

International Standard Book Number: 978-0-7884-4285-6

WRIGHT FAMILY

CENSUS RECORDS

APPOMATTOX COUNTY, VIRGINIA

1850 to 1900

Revised as of March 25, 2006

This document is an appendix to a larger work titled Sorting Some Of The Wrights Of Southern Virginia. The work is divided into parts for each family of Wrights that has been researched. Each part is divided into two sections; the first section is text discussing the family and the evidence supporting the relationships and the second section is a descendants chart summarizing the relationships and information known about each individual.

The appendices to the work (of which this document is one) present source records for persons named Wright by county and by type of record with the identification of the person named and their Wright ancestors to the extent known.

The sources for the records listed in this appendix are the following:

1) 1850 Census, Appomattox County, Virginia, available on Reel 933, Sutro Library, San Francisco, California and microfilm copy available from the National Archives, Pacific Sierra Region, 1000 Commodore Drive, San Bruno, California 94066.

2) 1850 Census Of Appomattox County, Virginia, compiled and published by Stuart McDearmon Farrar, P.O. Box 1142, Pamplin City, Virginia 23958, 1975.

3) 1860 Census, Appomattox County, Virginia, microfilm copy available from the National Archives, Pacific Sierra Region, 1000 Commodore Drive, San Bruno, California 94066.

4) 1860 Census, Appomattox County, Virginia, available on Reel 933, Sutro Library, San Francisco, California.

5) 1860 Census Of Appomattox County, Virginia, compiled and published by Stuart McDearmon Farrar, P.O. Box 1142, Pamplin City, Virginia 23958, 1984.

6)   870 Census Appomattox County, Virginia, microfilm copy available from the National Archives, Pacific Sierra Region, 1000 Commondore Drive, San Bruno, California 94066.

7) 1880 Census, Appomattox County, Virginia, microfilm copy available at the Sutro Library, San Francisco, California.

8) 1900 Census for Appomattox County, Virginia, microfilm copy available from the National Archives, Pacific Sierra Region, 1000 Commodore Drive, San Bruno, California 94066.

The identification of a person or their ancestor by year and county indicates their year of death and county of residence at death. For example, "1763 Thomas Wright of Bedford County" indicates that this was the Thomas Wright who died in 1763 in Bedford County. If no state is listed after the county, the state is Virginia; counties in states other than Virginia will have a state listed after the county, as in "1876 William S. Wright of Highland County, Ohio".

0128(032506)

A parenthetical after the name indicates an identification of the person when a place of death is not yet known, as in "John Wright (Goochland County Carpenter)". A county in parentheses after the name indicates the county with which that person was most identified when no evidence of the place of death has yet been found, as in "Grief Wright (Bedford County)".

All or portions of the text and descendants charts for each Wright family identified are available from the author:

Robert N. Grant
15 Campo Bello Court   (H) 650-854-0895
Menlo Park, California 94025   (O) 650-614-3800

This is a work in progress and I would be most interested in receiving additional information about any of the persons identified in these records in order to correct any errors or expand on the information given.

1850 CENSUS

APPOMATTOX COUNTY, VIRGINIA

Revised as of August 29, 2005

Appendix: Appomattox County, Virginia, 1850 Census

Name	Age	Sex	Color	Occupation	Value of Real Estate	Place of Birth	Married Within Year	Attended School Within Year	Cannot Read & Write	Dumb Blind Insane etc.	Identification
p.157 07/25/1850											
023											
Thomas P. Wright	29	M		Farmer		Virginia					
Amanda E. Wright	28	F				Virginia					
Caroline W. Wright	5	F				Virginia					
Thomas O. P. Wright	3	M				Virginia					
Adelia R. Wright	1	F				Virginia					
042											
Christian F. Johnson	50	M				Virginia					
Philip Johnson	77	M		None		Virginia					
Anderson D. Johnson	43	M		Farmer		Virginia					
Ann C. Wright	15	F				Virginia					
Martha J. Wright	11	F				Virginia					
052											
John M. Wright	33	M		Farmer & Miller	$1,550	Virginia					John M. Wright (Lunenburg County)
Emilia A. Wright	32	F				Virginia					
Thomas W. Wright	12	M				Virginia					
Christopher C. Wright	11	M				Virginia					
Emilia M. Wright	7	F				Virginia					
William R. Wright	4	M				Virginia					
Mary E. Wright	9	F				Virginia		1			
Charles F. Gunter(?)	25	M				Virginia					

Appendix: Appomattox County, Virginia, 1850 Census

Name	Age	Sex	Color	Occupation	Value of Real Estate	Place of Birth	Married Within Year	Attended School Within Year	Cannot Read & Write	Dumb Blind Insane etc.	Identification
p. 161 08/02/1850											
083											
James S. Wright	35	M		Farmer		Virginia					
Judith Wright	35	F				Virginia					
James A. Wright	11	M				Virginia		1			
Lucy J. Wright	10	F				Virginia		1			
John Burks	40	M		Laborer		Virginia					
Jane Wright	77	F				Virginia					
p. 163 08/03/1850											
110											
Samuel T. Wright	36	M		Farmer		Virginia					Samuel T. Wright, son of 1854 Samuel A. Wright of Appomattox County, grandson of 1820 Pryor Wright, Sr., of Prince Edward County, and great grandson of 1779 John Wright of Prince Edward County
Mary J. Wright	33	F				Virginia					
p. 165 08/05/1850											
154											
William W. Wright	28	M		Farmer	$800	Virginia					1881 William P. Wright of Appomattox County, son of Charles Wright and grandson of Robert Wright, Sr. (Campbell County)
William P. Wright	50	M		Laborer		Virginia					
Richard T. Wright	28	M		Laborer		Virginia					

Appendix: Appomattox County, Virginia, 1850 Census

Name	Age	Sex	Color	Occupation	Value of Real Estate	Place of Birth	Married Within Year	Attended School Within Year	Cannot Read & Write	Dumb Blind Insane etc.	Identification

p. 166 08/08/1850

171

Name	Age	Sex	Color	Occupation	Value of Real Estate	Place of Birth	Married Within Year	Attended School Within Year	Cannot Read & Write	Dumb Blind Insane etc.	Identification
Pryor B. Wright	48	M		Farmer		Virginia					1882 Pryor B. Wright of Appomattox County,
Lucinda P. Wright	48	F				Virginia					son of 1854 Samuel A. Wright of Appomattox
Mary J. Wright	23	F				Virginia					County, grandson of 1820 Pryor Wright, Sr., of
Saunders F. Wright	22	M		Laborer		Virginia					Prince Edward County, and great grandson of
Caswell C. Wright	20	M		Laborer		Virginia					1779 John Wright of Prince Edward County
Claudius F. Wright	15	M				Virginia		1			
Cornelius A. Wright	13	M				Virginia					
Lucinda P. Wright	12	F				Virginia		1			
Arissa C. Wright	10	F				Virginia		1			
Nancy C. Wright	8	F				Virginia					
Robert P. Wright	6	M				Virginia					
Barbary F. Wright	4	F				Virginia					

p. 167 08/09/1850

187

Name	Age	Sex	Color	Occupation	Value of Real Estate	Place of Birth	Married Within Year	Attended School Within Year	Cannot Read & Write	Dumb Blind Insane etc.	Identification
George A. Wright	52	M		Farmer	$1200	Virginia					1879 George Anderson Wright of Campbell
Elizabeth F. Wright	38	F				Virginia					County, son of 1811 John Wright of Campbell
Geo. W. Wright	2	M				Virginia					County and grandson of Robert Wright, Sr. (Campbell County)

190

Name	Age	Sex	Color	Occupation	Value of Real Estate	Place of Birth	Married Within Year	Attended School Within Year	Cannot Read & Write	Dumb Blind Insane etc.	Identification
Sarah A. Hamner	58	F			$1,100	Virginia					
Mary A. Wright	15	F				Virginia					
Mary B. Chambers	17	F				Virginia					

Appendix: Appomattox County, Virginia, 1850 Census

Name	Age	Sex	Color	Occupation	Value of Real Estate	Place of Birth	Married Within Year	Attended School Within Year	Cannot Read & Write	Dumb Blind Insane etc.	Identification
p. 171 08/13/1850											
246											
Joseph Grow	35	M		Collier		Virginia					
Eliza Grow	30	F				Virginia					
Lucy A. Grow	15	F				Virginia					
Joseph H. Grow	13	M				Virginia					
William Grow	11	M				Virginia					
Sarah F. Grow	9	F				Virginia					
Clinton Grow	8	M				Virginia					
Isabella Grow	6	F				Virginia					
Susan Grow	2	F				Virginia					
Robert Wright	40	M		Miner		Virginia					
Andrew J. Morris	23	M		Miner		Virginia					
Henry Rodenhiser	23	M		Founderer		Maryland					
John Kinear	20	M		Teamster		Virginia					
Washington Hudson	28	M		Teamster		Virginia					
William Wright	16	M				Virginia					
Washington F. Plunkett	26	M		Iron Master		Virginia					
Jesse T. Hutcheson	25	M		Iron Master		Virginia					
p. 172 08/13/1850											
260											
Wilson M. Wright	46	M		Farmer		Virginia					1882 Wilson M. Wright of Mercer County, West Virginia, son of 1823 George Wright of Campbell County and grandson of Robert Wright, Sr. (Campbell County)
Elizabeth Wright	46	F				Virginia					
Cassandale(?) E. Wright	24	F				Virginia					
Angeline A. Wright	22	F				Virginia					
Nancy J. Wright	18	F				Virginia					
Catharine A. Wright	15	F				Virginia					
James D. Wright	51	M		Laborer		Virginia					

Name	Age	Sex	Color	Occupation	Value of Real Estate	Place of Birth	Married Within Year	Attended School Within Year	Cannot Read & Write	Dumb Blind Insane etc.	Identification
p. 174 08/15/1850											
294											
Daniel P. Wright	49	M		Carpenter	$100	Virginia					Daniel P. Wright, son of 1811 John Wright of
Elizabeth Wright	48	F				Virginia					Campbell County and grandson of Robert
William P. Wright	25	M		Carpenter		Virginia					Wright, Sr. (Campbell County)
Cynthia A. Wright	21	F				Virginia					
Elizabeth Wright	19	F				Virginia					
Robert Wright	14	M				Virginia		1			
John D. Wright	11	M				Virginia		1			
Henry D. Wright	9	M				Virginia		1			
Mary A. Wright	5	F				Virginia					
Nancy M. Wright	3	F				Virginia					
p. 175											
299											
John A. Phelps	48	M		Farmer	$750	Virginia					
Nancy Phelps	36	F				Virginia					
Thomas Wright	57	M		Laborer		Virginia					
p. 176 08/17/1850											
321											
Campbell S. Wright	23	M		Shoemaker		Virginia					Campbell S. Wright, son of 1854 Pryor Rucker
Mildred A. Wright	28	F				Virginia					Wright, Jr., of Appomattox County, grandson of
Mariah J. Wright	4	F				Virginia					1820 Pryor Wright, Sr., of Prince Edward
Harris C. Wright	1	M				Virginia					County, and great grandson of 1779 John
Frederick R. Durham	9	M				Virginia		1			Wright of Prince Edward County
Walker Durham	6	M				Virginia		1			
John R. Durham	5	M				Virginia		1			

Appendix: Appomattox County, Virginia, 1850 Census

Name	Age	Sex	Color	Occupation	Value of Real Estate	Place of Birth	Married Within Year	Attended School Within Year	Cannot Read & Write	Dumb Blind Insane etc.	Identification
p. 177 08/17/1850											
326											
Pryor Wright	60	M		Farmer	$3000	Virginia					1854 Pryor Rucker Wright, Jr., of Appomattox
Marriah Wright	38	F				Virginia					County, son of 1820 Pryor Wright, Sr., of Prince
Leanirs J. Wright	16	M		Laborer		Virginia					Edward County and grandson of 1779 John
Fountain C. Wright	9	M				Virginia					Wright of Prince Edward County
Gilliam Wright	7	M				Virginia					
Chambers L. Wright	5	M				Virginia					
329											
Robert J. Wright	32	M		Blacksmith		Virginia					Robert J. Wright, possibly son of 1854
Jane Wright	36	F				Virginia					Samuel A. Wright of Appomattox County,
Cuzzy Wright	6	F				Virginia					grandson of 1820 Pryor Wright, Sr., of Prince
William Wright	4	M				Virginia					Edward County, and great grandson of 1779 John Wright of Prince Edward County
p. 180 08/21/1850											
375											
Robert B. Wright	45	M		Farmer		Virginia					Robert B. Wright, son of 1815 Robert C. Wright
Kezziah Wright	43	F				Virginia					of Prince Edward County, grandson of 1820
Columbus H. Wright	19	M		Laborer		Virginia					Pryor Wright, Sr., of Prince Edward County, and
Malissa A. Wright	17	F				Virginia		1			great grandson of 1779 John Wright of Prince
Euclid Wright	13	M				Virginia					Edward County
Mary F. Wright	13	F				Virginia		1			
Ovid B. Wright	1	M				Virginia					

Appendix: Appomattox County, Virginia, 1850 Census

Name	Age	Sex	Color	Occupation	Value of Real Estate	Place of Birth	Married Within Year	Attended School Within Year	Cannot Read & Write	Dumb Blind Insane etc.	Identification
p. 184 08/22/1850											
428											
Samuel A. Wright	73	M		Farmer	$1200	Virginia					1854 Samuel A. Wright of Appomattox County,
Barbary G. Wright	70	F				Virginia					son of 1820 Pryor Wright, Sr., of Prince Edward
Crosby Wright	35	F				Virginia					County and grandson of 1779 John Wright of
Barbary G. Wright	30	F				Virginia					Prince Edward County
Loving A. Wright	30	M				Virginia					
p. 186 08/27/1850											
448											
William M. Wright	39	M		Farmer	$1000	Virginia					1897 William M. Wright of Bedford County, son
Martha Wright	42	F				Virginia					of 1854 Samuel A. Wright of Appomattox
Samuel A. Wright	12	M				Virginia		1			County, grandson of 1820 Pryor Wright, Sr., of
Marian North	18	F				Virginia					Prince Edward County, and great grandson of 1779 John Wright of Prince Edward County
p. 196 9/5/1850											
395											
Thomas S. Wright	37	M		Merchant		Virginia					1883 Thomas Smith Wright of Campbell County,
Elizabeth Wright	30	F				Virginia					son of 1842 Thomas Wright of Buckingham
John J. Wright	9	M				Virginia		1			County
William A. Wright	8	M				Virginia		1			
Frances Wright	5	F				Virginia					
Benjamin Wright	2	M				Virginia					
Mary S. Wright	9/12	F				Virginia					

1860 CENSUS

APPOMATTOX COUNTY, VIRGINIA

Revised as of August 29, 2005

Appendix: Appomattox County, Virginia, 1860 Census

Name	Age	Sex	Color	Occupation	Value of Real Estate	Value of Personal Property	Place of Birth	Married Within Year	Attended School Within Year	Cannot Read & Write	Deaf Dumb Blind Insane etc.	Identification
194/194 07/05/1860												
Claudius I. Wright	26	M		Farmer		$30	Virginia			1		Claudius F. Wright, son of 1882 Pryor B. Wright of Appomattox County, grandson of 1854 Samuel A. Wright of Appomattox County and grandson of 1815 Robert C. Wright of Prince Edward County, great grandson of 1820 Pryor Wright, Sr., of Prince Edward County, and great great grandson of 1779 John Wright of Prince Edward County
Martha Wright	22	F		Wife			Virginia			1		
Willie A. Wright	3	F					Virginia					
Thomas H. Wright	10/12	M					Virginia					
248/248 07/13/1860												
Campbell S. Wright	32	M		Shoemaker	$150	$100	Virginia					Campbell S. Wright, son of 1854 Pryor Rucker Wright, Jr., of Apomattox County, grandson of 1820 Pryor Wright, Sr., of Prince Edward County, and great grandson of 1779 John Wright of Prince Edward County
Mildred A. Wright	39	F		Wife			Virginia			1		
Mariah J. Wright	13	F					Virginia		1			
Virginia A. Wright	8	F					Virginia					
Nancy C. Wright	2	F					Virginia					

Appendix: Appomattox County, Virginia, 1860 Census

Name	Age	Sex	Color	Occupation	Value of Real Estate	Value of Personal Property	Place of Birth	Married Within Year	Attended School Within Year	Cannot Read & Write	Deaf Dumb Blind Insane etc.	Identification
365/365 08/03/1860												
Loving A. Wright	39	M		Farmer	$100	$200	Virginia					Loving A. Wright, son of 1854
Martha L. Wright	28	F		Wife			Virginia			1		Samuel A. Wright of
George W. A. Wright	6	M					Virginia		1			Appomattox County, grandson
Kiziah B. Wright	4	F					Virginia					of 1820 Pryor Wright, Sr., of
Saml A. Wright	2	M					Virginia					Prince Edward County, and
Jemima Wright	3/12	F					Virginia					great grandson of 1779 John
Mrs. Ann Fore	62	F					Virginia			1		Wright of Prince Edward County
Susan E. Fore	21	F					Virginia					
John A. Fore	17	M					Virginia					
Martha E. Fore	1	F					Virginia					
392/392 08/07/1860												
Pryor B. Wright	57	M		Farmer	$1200	$3750	Virginia					1882 Pryor B. Wright of
Lucinda P. Wright	57	F		Wife			Virginia			1		Appomattox County, son of
Mary J. Wright	35	F					Virginia					1854 Samuel A. Wright of
Saunders F. Wright	33	M		Farmer	$500		Virginia					Appomattox County, grandson
Caswell C. Wright	29	M		Laborer			Virginia					of 1820 Pryor Wright, Sr. of
Cornelius C. Wright	26	M		Laborer			Virginia					Prince Edward County and
Lucinda P. Wright	23	F					Virginia					great grandson of 1779 John
Arissa C. Wright	20	F					Virginia					Wright of Prince Edward County
Nancy C. Wright	17	F					Virginia					
Barbary F. Wright	11	F					Virginia					
Robt P. Wright	14	M					Virginia					

Appendix: Appomattox County, Virginia, 1860 Census

Name	Age	Sex	Color	Occupation	Value of Real Estate	Value of Personal Property	Place of Birth	Married Within Year	Attended School Within Year	Cannot Read & Write	Deaf Dumb Blind Insane etc.	Identification
426/426 08/11/1860												
Mrs. Mariah Wright (W)	43	F		Farmer	$1000	$3000	Virginia					Mariah (Turner) (Wright) Webb, widow of 1854 Pryor Rucker Wright, Jr., of Apomattox County, a son of 1820 Pryor Wright, Sr., of Prince Edward County and grandson of 1779 John Wright of Prince Edward County
John A. Rosser	30	M		Buggy Maker	$85	$185	Virginia					
Sarah J. Wright	7	F					Virginia		1			
Lenis T. Rosser	24	F		Wife			Virginia					
539/539 08/29/1860												
James A. Wright	21	M		Grocer		$500	Virginia					
571/571 08/30/1860												
Wm. W. Wright	40	M		Tenant		$300	Virginia			1		William Wesley Wright
Susan F. Wright	26	F		Wife			Virginia			1		
John W. Wright	10	M					Virginia		1			
Nancy Wright	8	F					Virginia					
Thomas H. Wright	6	M					Virginia					
Wm. F. Wright	5	M					Virginia					
Elizabeth S. Wright	3	F					Virginia					
Mary F. Wright	5/12	F					Virginia					
Mrs. Mary Wright	65	F					Virginia					

Appendix: Appomattox County, Virginia, 1860 Census

Name	Age	Sex	Color	Occupation	Value of Real Estate	Value of Personal Property	Place of Birth	Married Within Year	Attended School Within Year	Cannot Read & Write	Deaf Dumb Blind Insane etc.	Identification
582/582 08/21/1860												
Benjamin E. Wright	34	M		Farmer		$600	Virginia					1880 Benjamin Edward Wright
Mary F. Wright	29	F		Wife			Virginia					of Amherst County, son of 1881
Luther W. Wright	8	M					Virginia		1			William P. Wright of Appomattox
John W. Wright	6	M					Virginia		1			County, grandson of Charles
Charles W. Wright	5	M					Virginia					Wright, and great grandson of
Benjamin W. Wright	2	M					Virginia					Robert Wright, Sr. (Campbell
Mary Smith	18	F		Housekeeper			Virginia					County)
Wm. P. Wright	58	M		Retired farmer			Virginia					
606/606 09/04/1860												
Hector Phelps	52	M		Farmer	$2,300	$1120	Virginia					
Jane B. Phelps	56	F		Wife			Virginia					
Watkins L. Phelps	21	M		Laborer			Virginia					
Jas. M. Phelps	20	M		Laborer			Virginia					
Martha Smith	35	F		Housekeeper			Virginia					
Jno. Burks	50	M					Virginia					
Phoebe Wright (W)	85	F		W. of War 1812			Virginia					
670/670 09/12/1860												
John L. Turner	39	M		Tenant Farmer		$12,000	Virginia					Fielding Hobson Wright, son of
Mary E. Turner	38	F		Wife			Virginia					1873 Robert D. Wright of
Rosa A. Turner	7	F					Virginia					Amherst County, grandson of
Sarah E. Turner	5	F					Virginia					Charles Wright, and great
Mary S. Turner	3	F					Virginia					grandson of Robert Wright, Sr.
Fielding A. Wright	36	M		Overseer			Virginia					(Campbell County)
George E. Baily	17	M		Laborer			Virginia					

Appendix: Appomattox County, Virginia, 1860 Census

Name	Age	Sex	Color	Occupation	Value of Real Estate	Value of Personal Property	Place of Birth	Married Within Year	Attended School Within Year	Cannot Read & Write	Deaf Dumb Blind Insane etc.	Identification
690/690 09/13/1860												
Wm. W. Wright	39	M		Farmer	$800	$255	Virginia			1		William Washington Wright, son
Elizabeth I. Wright	23	F		Wife			Virginia					of 1881 William P. Wright of
Richard T. Wright	36	M		Laborer			Virginia					Appomattox County, grandson
Robert B. Wright	5	M					Virginia					of Charles Wright, and great
Silia F. Wright	1	F					Virginia					grandson of Robert Wright, Sr.
David M. Wright	29	M		Laborer			Virginia					(Campbell County)

1870 CENSUS

APPOMATTOX COUNTY, VIRGINIA

Revised as of February 12, 2005

Name	Age	Sex	Color	Occupation	Value of Real Estate	Value of Personal Property	Place of Birth	Married Within Year	Born Within Year	Attended School Within Year	Cannot Read	Cannot Write	Deaf Dumb Blind Insane or or Idiot
378/378 07/14/1870													
Saunders Wright	38	M	W	Farmer	600	400	East Va						
405/405 07/15/1870													
Pryor B Wright	66	M	W	Farmer	1000	150	E. Va						
Lucinda P Wright	66	F	W	Keeping House			E. Va						
Mary J Wright	35	F	W	At Home			E. Va						
Lucinda P. Wright	21	F	W	At Home			E. Va						
Aritha W. Wright	20	F	W	At Home			E. Va						
Fannie Wright	17	F	W	At Home			E. Va						
406/406 07/15/1870													
Claudius Wright	30	M	W	Farm Laborer			E. Va						
Martha Wright	28	F	W	Keeping House			E. Va						
Willis Wright	12	M	W				E. Va						
Thomas Wright	10	M	W				E. Va						
Nancy B. Wright	7	F	W				E. Va						
Caswel Wright	1	M	W				E. Va						
431/431 07/15/1870													
Campbell C Wright	38	M	W	Shoemaker			E. Va						
Mildred A Wright	48	F	W	Keeping House			E. Va						
Nancy Wright	14	F	W	Seamstress			E. Va						

Appendix: Appomattox County, Virginia, 1870 Census

Name [Continued from prior page]	Male Citizen Over 21	Male Citizen Over 21 Without Right to Vote	Identification
378/378 07/14/1870			
Saunders Wright	1		Saunders F. Wright, son of 1882 Pryor B. Wright of Appomattox County, grandson of 1854 Samuel A. Wright of Appomattox County, great grandson of 1820 Pryor Wright, Sr., of Prince Edward County, and great great grandson of 1779 John Wright of Prince Edward County
405/405 07/15/1870			
Pryor B Wright Lucinda P Wright Mary J Wright Lucinda P. Wright Aritha W. Wright Fannie Wright	1		1882 Pryor B. Wright of Appomattox County, son of 1854 Samuel A. Wright of Appomattox County, grandson of 1820 Pryor Wright, Sr., of Prince Edward County, and great grandson of 1779 John Wright of Prince Edward County
406/406 07/15/1870			
Claudius Wright Martha Wright Willis Wright Thomas Wright Nancy B. Wright Caswel Wright	1		Claudius or Collodius F. Wright son of 1882 Pryor B. Wright of Appomattox County, grandson of 1854 Samuel A. Wright of Appomattox County, great grandson of 1820 Pryor Wright, Sr., of Prince Edward County, and great great grandson of 1779 John Wright of Prince Edward County
431/431 07/15/1870			
Campbell C Wright Mildred A Wright Nancy Wright	1		Campbell S. Wright, son of 1854 Pryor Rucker Wright, Jr., of Appomattox County, grandson of 1820 Pryor Wright, Sr., of Prince Edward County, and great grandson of 1779 John Wright of Prince Edward County

Appendix: Appomattox County, Virginia, 1870 Census

Name	Age	Sex	Color	Occupation	Value of Real Estate	Value of Personal Property	Place of Birth	Married Within Year	Born Within Year	Attended School Within Year	Cannot Read	Cannot Write	Deaf Dumb Blind Insane or or Idiot

471/471 07/18/1870

Name	Age	Sex	Color	Occupation	Value of Real Estate	Value of Personal Property	Place of Birth	Married Within Year	Born Within Year	Attended School Within Year	Cannot Read	Cannot Write	Deaf Dumb Blind Insane or or Idiot
York Wright	50	M	B	Blacksmith	650	150	E. Va					1	
Ann Wright	38	F	B	Keeping H			E. Va					1	
Henry Wright	24	M	B	Laborer			E. Va					1	
Benjamin Wright	19	M	B	Striker in shop			E. Va					1	
William Wright	15	M	B	Farm Laborer			E. Va				1	1	
Birelia A. Wright	13	F	B	Seamstress			E. Va						
Casey B Wright	9	M	B				E. Va						
York N Wright	8	M	B				E. Va						
Eliza Jane	4	F	B				E. Va						
George G. Wright	2	M	B				E. Va						

488/488 07/18/1870

Name	Age	Sex	Color	Occupation	Value of Real Estate	Value of Personal Property	Place of Birth	Married Within Year	Born Within Year	Attended School Within Year	Cannot Read	Cannot Write	Deaf Dumb Blind Insane or or Idiot
Henry Wright	22	M	B	Laborer			E. Va					1	
Susan Wright	22	F	B	Keeping H			E. Va				1	1	
Victoria Wright	8	F	B				E. Va						
Mary Wright	4	F	B				E. Va						
Charles Wright	3	M	B				E. Va						
Davy Wright	11/12	M	B				E. Va		Sept				

609/609 07/22/1870

Name	Age	Sex	Color	Occupation	Value of Real Estate	Value of Personal Property	Place of Birth	Married Within Year	Born Within Year	Attended School Within Year	Cannot Read	Cannot Write	Deaf Dumb Blind Insane or or Idiot
Wm Cotrell	27	M	B	Farmer	400	400	Virginia				1	1	
Mary A Cottrell	30	F	B	Keeping H			Virginia				1	1	
Mary J Cotrell	2	F	B				Virginia						
Martha Johnson	14	F	B	At Home			Virginia						
Martha A Johnson	51	F	B	Not employ			Virginia				1	1	
Willard A. Cotrell	18	M	B	F. L.			Virginia				1	1	
Reubin Wright	12	M	B	F. L.			Virginia						

Appendix: Appomattox County, Virginia, 1870 Census

Name [Continued from prior page]	Male Citizen Over 21	Male Citizen Over 21 Without Right to Vote	Identification
481/481 07/18/1870			
York Wright	1		1880 York Wright of Appomattox County
Ann Wright	1		
Henry Wright	1		
Benjamin Wright			
William Wright			
Birelia A. Wright			
Casey B Wright			
York N Wright			
Eliza Jane			
George G. Wright			
488/488 07/18/1870			
Henry Wright	1		
Susan Wright			
Victoria Wright			
Mary Wright			
Charles Wright			
Davy Wright			
609/609 07/22/1870			
Wm Cotrell	1		
Mary A Cottrell			
Mary J Cotrell			
Martha Johnson			
Martha A Johnson			
Willard A. Cotrell			
Reubin Wright			

Appendix: Appomattox County, Virginia, 1870 Census

Name	Age	Sex	Color	Occupation	Value of Real Estate	Value of Personal Property	Place of Birth	Married Within Year	Born Within Year	Attended School Within Year	Cannot Read	Cannot Write	Deaf Dumb Blind Insane or or Idiot
684/684 07/25/1870													
Cornelius Wright	35	M	W	Farmer	600	121	E Va						
Maria L. Wright	30	F	W	Keep H			E Va						
Bradford Wright	2	M	W				E Va						
685/685 07/26/1870													
Anderson Johnson	68	M	W	F. Laborer			Virginia						
Christiana P Johnson	(?)	F	W	Keeping House			Va						
Ann C. Wright	35	F	W	Keep H.			Va						
Cornelia Wright	12	F	W	At school			Va			1			
Christopher Wright	10	M	W	At school			Va			1			
Alice C. Wright	4	F	W				Va						
009/009 09/01/1870													
Louis Patterson	33	M	B	R. R. Laborer			Virginia				1	1	
Mary Patterson	29	F	B	Keeping House			Va						
Sarah Ella Patterson	12	F	B	At home			Va						
Taylor Wright	29	M	B	Farm Laborer			Va				1	1	
356/356 17/09/1870													
James R Wright	42	M	W	Lawyer		150	Va						
Sarah E Wright	38	F	W	Keeping House			Va						
Hattie Wright	16	F	W	Attending School			Va			1			
James Wright	12	M	W	attending school			Va			1			
John W Wright	10	M	W	attending School			Va			1			
Bettie S Wright	8	F	W				Va						
William Wright	6	M	W				Va						
Capella Wright	9/12	F	W				Va		Sept				

Appendix: Appomattox County, Virginia, 1870 Census

Name [Continued from prior page]	Male Citizen Over 21	Male Citizen Over 21 Without Right to Vote	Identification
684/684 07/25/1870			
Cornelius Wright Maria L. Wright Bradford Wright	1		Cornelius A. Wright, son of 1882 Pryor B. Wright of Appomattox County, grandson of 1854 Samuel A. Wright of Appomattox County, great grandson of 1820 Pryor Wright, Sr., of Prince Edward County, and great great grandson of 1779 John Wright of Prince Edward County
685/685 07/26/1870			
Anderson Johnson Christiana P Johnson Ann C. Wright Cornelia Wright Christopher Wright Alice C. Wright	1		
009/009 09/01/1870			
Louis Patterson Mary Patterson Sarah Ella Patterson Taylor Wright	1 1		
356/356 17/09/1870			
James R Wright Sarah E Wright Hattie Wright James Wright John W Wright Bettie S Wright William Wright Capella Wright	1		

Name	Age	Sex	Color	Occupation	Value of Real Estate	Value of Personal Property	Place of Birth	Married Within Year	Born Within Year	Attended School Within Year	Cannot Read	Cannot Write	Deaf Dumb Blind Insane or or Idiot
151/151 08/06/1870													
Thos J Nowlin	24	M	B	Farm Laborer			E. Va				1	1	
Mary V Nowlin	23	F	B				E. Va						
Lucy M Nowlin	4	F	B				E. Va						
Susanna Nowlin	2	F	B				E. Va						
Thomas Edward Nowlin	2/12	M	B				E. Va						
William Wright	13	M	M				E. Va						
154/154 08/08/1870													
Wm W. Wright	42	M	W	Farmer	800	300	E. Va						
Elizabeth Wright	34	F	W	Keeping House			E. Va						
Robert B Wright	15	M	W	Laborer			E. Va						
Lelice F Wright	11	F	W	House			E. Va						
Mary H Wright	9	F	W				E. Va						
Dora Ann Wright	7	F	W				E. Va						
Martha C. Wright	4	F	W				E. Va						
Sarah B. Wright	1	F	W				E. Va						
Susan Giles	68	F	W	At Home			E. Va						
Richard H. Wright	42	M	W	Laborer on F.			E. Va						
426/426 08/20/1870													
Philis Wright	45	F	B	Keeping House			Va				1	1	
Henry Wright	19	M	B	Farm Laborer			Va				1	1	
Washington Wright	17	M	B	Farm Laborer			Va				1	1	
Frank Wright	13	M	B	Farm Laborer			Va				1	1	

Appendix: Appomattox County, Virginia, 1870 Census

Name [Continued from prior page]	Male Citizen Over 21	Male Citizen Over 21 Without Right to Vote	Identification
151/151 08/06/1870			
Thos J Nowlin	1		
Mary V Nowlin			
Lucy M Nowlin			
Susanna Nowlin			
Thomas Edward Nowlin			
William Wright	1		
154/154 08/08/1870			
Wm W. Wright	1		William Washington Wright, son of 1881 William P. Wright of Appomattox County, grandson of Charles Wright, and great grandson of Robert Wright, Sr. (Campbell County)
Elizabeth Wright			
Robert B Wright			
Lelice F Wright			
Mary H Wright			
Dora Ann Wright			
Martha C. Wright			
Sarah B. Wright			
Susan Giles			
Richard H. Wright	1		
426/426 08/20/1870			
Philis Wright			
Henry Wright			
Washington Wright			
Frank Wright			

0128(032506)

1880 CENSUS

APPOMATOX COUNTY, VIRGINIA

Revised as of February 12, 2005

Appendix: Appomattox County, Virginia, 1880 Census

Name	Color	Sex	Age	Month of Birth	Relationship	Marital Status	Married During Year	Occupation	Months Unem- ployed	Sickness Blind Deaf & Dumb Idiotic Disabled

Clover Hill Magisterial District
June 1, 1880

Dwelling #7/Family #7

Name	Color	Sex	Age	Month of Birth	Relationship	Marital Status	Married During Year	Occupation	Months Unemployed	Sickness
Augusta Anne Wright	B	F	46			W		Keeping house		
Henry Wright	B	M	30		Son	S		at home		
Elisa Jane Wright	B	F	15		daughter	S		at home		
York Wright	B	M	16		Son	S		laborer		
George Wright	B	M	11		Son	S		laborer		
Alexander Wright	B	M	9		Son	S				

June 2, 1880

Dwelling #24/Family #24

Name	Color	Sex	Age	Month of Birth	Relationship	Marital Status	Married During Year	Occupation	Months Unemployed	Sickness
Henry Wright	W	M	28			M		Farmer		
Maria L Wright	W	F	25		Wife	M		Keeping House		
Mary Anne Wright	W	F	7		Daughter	S				
William Henry Wright	W	M	6		Son	S				
Martine Wright	W	F	4		Daughter	S				
Elisabeth Wright	W	F	2		Daughter	S				
Infant Wright	W	F	3/12		Daughter	S				

Appendix: Appomattox County, Virginia, 1880 Census

Name continued from previous page]	Attended School Within Year	Cannot Read	Cannot Write	Born	Father Born	Mother Born	Identification
Clover Hill Magisterial District							
June 1, 1880							
Dwelling #7/Family #7							
Augusta Anne Wright			1	Virginia	Virginia	Virginia	Augusta Anne (____) Wright, widow of 1880 York Wright of Appomattox County
Henry Wright			1	Virginia	Virginia	Virginia	
Elisa Jane Wright			1	Virginia	Virginia	Virginia	
York Wright		1	1	Virginia	Virginia	Virginia	
George Wright				Virginia	Virginia	Virginia	
Alexander Wright				Virginia	Virginia	Virginia	
June 2, 1880							
Dwelling #24/Family #24							
Henry Wright		1	1	Virginia	Virginia	Virginia	
Maria L Wright			1	Virginia	Virginia	Virginia	
Mary Anne Wright				Virginia	Virginia	Virginia	
William Henry Wright				Virginia	Virginia	Virginia	
Martine Wright				Virginia	Virginia	Virginia	
Elisabeth Wright				Virginia	Virginia	Virginia	
Infant Wright				Virginia	Virginia	Virginia	

Appendix: Appomattox County, Virginia, 1880 Census

Name	Color	Sex	Age	Month of Birth	Relationship	Marital Status	Married During Year	Occupation	Months Unem- ployed	Sickness Blind Deaf & Dumb Idiotic Disabled

June 9, 1880

Dwelling #146/Family #146

Name	Color	Sex	Age	Month of Birth	Relationship	Marital Status	Married During Year	Occupation	Months Unemployed	Sickness
Jim Wright	B	M	40			M		Farm tenant		
Jane Wright	B	F	30		Wife	M		Keeping House		
Marey Wright	B	F	18		daughter	S		at Home		
Betty Wright	B	F	16		Daughter	S		at Home		
Clara Belle Wright	B	F	7		Daughter	S		at Home		
Willis Wright	B	M	5		son	S				
Infant Wright	B	M	4/12		son	S				
Robert Davidson	B	M	23		Bro in law	S		laborer		

June 10, 1880

Dwelling #163/Family #163

Name	Color	Sex	Age	Month of Birth	Relationship	Marital Status	Married During Year	Occupation	Months Unemployed	Sickness
Jno B Pankey	W	M	27			M		Merchant & Notary Public		
Sarah Pankey	W	F	18		Wife	M		Keeping House		
Allen Pankey	W	M	2		Son	S				
Lucy Pankey	W	F	1		daughter	S				
Dooda Wright	B	F	23		Servant	S		Servant		

Appendix: Appomattox County, Virginia, 1880 Census

Name continued from previous page]	Attended School Within Year	Cannot Read	Cannot Write	Born	Father Born	Mother Born	Identification
June 9, 1880							
Dwelling #146/Family #146							
Jim Wright		1	1	Virginia	Virginia	Virginia	
Jane Wright		1	1	Virginia	Virginia	Virginia	
Marey Wright	1		1	Virginia	Virginia	Virginia	
Betty Wright			1	Virginia	Virginia	Virginia	
Clara Belle Wright				Virginia	Virginia	Virginia	
Willis Wright				Virginia	Virginia	Virginia	
Infant Wright				Virginia	Virginia	Virginia	
Robert Davidson			1	Virginia	Virginia	Virginia	
June 10, 1880							
Dwelling #163/Family #163							
Jno B Pankey				Virginia	Virginia	Virginia	
Sarah Pankey				Virginia	Virginia	Virginia	
Allen Pankey				Virginia	Virginia	Virginia	
Lucy Pankey				Virginia	Virginia	Virginia	
Dooda Wright			1	Virginia	Virginia	Virginia	

Name	Color	Sex	Age	Month of Birth	Relationship	Marital Status	Married During Year	Occupation	Months Unem-ployed	Sickness Blind Deaf & Dumb Idiotic Disabled

June 12, 1880

Dwelling #232/Family #232

Name	Color	Sex	Age	Month of Birth	Relationship	Marital Status	Married During Year	Occupation	Months Unem-ployed	Sickness etc.
Melinda Wright	Mu	F	45			W		Keeping House		
Mariettie Wright	Mu	F	30		daughter	W		at Home		
Sam Wright	Mu	M	23		son	S		farmer		
Beraregard Wright	Mu	M	19		son	S		laborer		
George Holman	Mu	M	12		Grandson	S		at Home		
Fanny Holman	Mu	F	10		Granddaughter	S		at Home		
James Wright	Mu	M	7		Grandson	S		at Home		
Charles Pearly(?)	Mu	M	5		Grandson	S		at Home		

Dwelling #234/Family #234

Name	Color	Sex	Age	Month of Birth	Relationship	Marital Status	Married During Year	Occupation	Months Unem-ployed	Sickness etc.
Benjamin Wright	B	M	28			M		Plantation Laborer		
Molly Wright	Mu	F	24		wife	M		Keeping House		
Agie F Wright	Mu	M	6		son	S				
____ Wright	Mu	F	3		daughter	S				
Lilly F Wright	Mu	F	1		daughter	S				
Willis T__	Mu	M	22		Border	S		Engineer(?)		

Appendix: Appomattox County, Virginia, 1880 Census

Name continued from previous page]	Attended School Within Year	Cannot Read	Cannot Write	Born	Father Born	Mother Born	Identification
June 12, 1880							
Dwelling #232/Family #232							
Melinda Wright		1	1	Virginia	Virginia	Virginia	
Mariettie Wright			1	Virginia	Virginia	Virginia	
Sam Wright				Virginia	Virginia	Virginia	
Beraregard Wright	1			Virginia	Virginia	Virginia	
George Holman	1			Virginia	Virginia	Virginia	
Fanny Holman	1		1	Virginia	Virginia	Virginia	
James Wright	1			Virginia	Virginia	Virginia	
Charles Pearly(?)				Virginia	Virginia	Virginia	
Dwelling #234/Family #234							
Benjamin Wright		1	1	Virginia	Virginia	Virginia	
Molly Wright		1	1	Virginia	Virginia	Virginia	
Agie F Wright	1			Virginia	Virginia	Virginia	
____ Wright				Virginia	Virginia	Virginia	
Lilly F Wright				Virginia	Virginia	Virginia	
Willis T__				Virginia	Virginia	Virginia	

Appendix: Appomattox County, Virginia, 1880 Census

Name	Color	Sex	Age	Month of Birth	Relationship	Marital Status	Married During Year	Occupation	Months Unemployed	Sickness Blind Deaf & Dumb Idiotic Disabled
June 9, 1880										
Dwelling #206/Family #206										
Saml R Habbard	W	M	53			M		Farmer		
Ann J Habbard	W	F	50		Wife	M		Keeping House		
John T Habbard	W	M	25		Son	S		farm laborer		
Willie Habbard	W	M	22		Son	S		farm laborer		
Samuel Habbard	W	M	18		Son	S		farm laborer		
Robert Habbard	W	M	15		son	S		farm laborer		
Walter Habbard	W	M	12		son	S		at school		
S L Wright	W	F	28		daughter	D		at Home		
Lucy Meek(?)	B	F	72		Servant	W		Servant		
June 11, 1880										
Dwelling #257/Family #257										
Geo T. Peen	W	M	49			M		Clerk Circuit County Court		
Virginia C Peen	W	F	42		wife	M		Keeping House		
Lelia S Peen	W	F	21		daughter	S		at Home		1
Charles S. Peen	W	M	16		Son	S		Student		
Lulu Peen	W	F	10		daughter	S		at School		
Mary Wright	Mu	F	15		Servant	S		Servant		

Name continued from previous page]	Attended School Within Year	Cannot Read	Cannot Write	Born	Father Born	Mother Born	Identification
June 9, 1880							
Dwelling #206/Family #206							
Saml R Habbard				Virginia	Virginia	Virginia	
Ann J Habbard				Virginia	Virginia	Virginia	
John T Habbard				Virginia	Virginia	Virginia	
Willie Habbard				Virginia	Virginia	Virginia	
Samuel Habbard				Virginia	Virginia	Virginia	
Robert Habbard				Virginia	Virginia	Virginia	
Walter Habbard	1			Virginia	Virginia	Virginia	
S L Wright				Virginia	Virginia	Virginia	
Lucy Meek(?)				Virginia	Virginia	Virginia	
June 11, 1880							
Dwelling #257/Family #257							
Geo T. Peen				Virginia	Va	Va	
Virginia C Peen				Tennessee	Massachusetts	Tennessee	
Lelia S Peen				Virginia	Virginia	Tennessee	
Charles S. Peen	1			Virginia	Virginia	Tennessee	
Lulu Peen	1			Virginia	Virginia	Tennessee	
Mary Wright		1	1	Virginia	Virginia	Tennessee	

Appendix: Appomattox County, Virginia, 1880 Census

Name	Color	Sex	Age	Month of Birth	Relationship	Marital Status	Married During Year	Occupation	Months Unemployed	Sickness Blind Deaf & Dumb Idiotic Disabled

June 14 & 16, 1880

Dwelling #305/Family #305

Name	Color	Sex	Age	Month of Birth	Relationship	Marital Status	Married During Year	Occupation	Months Unemployed	Sickness
Pryer B Wright	W	M	70			W		farmer		
Lucinda Wright	W	F	30		daughter	S		keeping House		
F. B. Wright	W	F	21		daughter	S		at Home		

June 22, 1880

Dwelling #427/Family #438

Name	Color	Sex	Age	Month of Birth	Relationship	Marital Status	Married During Year	Occupation	Months Unemployed	Sickness
Bertha Wright	B	F	25			M		Keeping House		
C__n Wright	B	F	6		Daughter	S				
Celia Wright	B	F	4		Daughter	S				
Infant Wright	B	F	May		Daughter	S				

June 24 & 25, 1880

Dwelling #476/Family #478

Name	Color	Sex	Age	Month of Birth	Relationship	Marital Status	Married During Year	Occupation	Months Unemployed	Sickness
Harry Wright	B	M	35			M		Farm laborer		
Susan Wright	B	F	33		wife	M		keeping House		
Victoria Wright	B	F	17		Daughter	S		working in the field		
Mary Wright	B	F	16		Daughter	S		"at Service"		
Charlie Wright	B	M	12		Son	S		working in the field		
David(?) Wright	B	M	9		Son	S				
Willie Wright	B	M	8		Son	S				
Lizzie Wright	B	F	6		Daughter	S				
Henry Wright	B	M	1		Son	S				

Appendix: Appomattox County, Virginia, 1880 Census

Name continued from previous page]	Attended School Within Year	Cannot Read	Cannot Write	Born	Father Born	Mother Born	Identification
June 14 & 16, 1880							
Dwelling #305/Family #305							
Pryer B Wright		1	1	Virginia	Va	Va	1882 Pryor B. Wright of Appomattox County, son of 1854
Lucinda Wright				Virginia	Va	Va	Samuel A. Wright of Appomattox County, grandson of 1820
F. B. Wright				Virginia	Va	Va	Pryor Wright, Sr., of Prince Edward County, and great grandson
							of 1779 John Wright of Prince Edward County
June 22, 1880							
Dwelling #427/Family #438							
Bertha Wright		1	1	Virginia	Va	Va	
C__n Wright				Virginia	Va	Va	
Celia Wright				Virginia	Va	Va	
Infant Wright				Virginia	Va	Va	
June 24 & 25, 1880							
Dwelling #476/Family #478							
Harry Wright		1	1	Virginia	Va	Va	
Susan Wright		1	1	Virginia	Va	Va	
Victoria Wright			1	Virginia	Va	Va	
Mary Wright		1	1	Virginia	Va	Va	
Charlie Wright	1		1	Virginia	Va	Va	
David(?) Wright				Virginia	Va	Va	
Willie Wright				Virginia	Va	Va	
Lizzie Wright				Virginia	Va	Va	
Henry Wright				Virginia	Va	Va	

Name	Color	Sex	Age	Month of Birth	Relationship	Marital Status	Married During Year	Occupation	Months Unem- ployed	Sickness Blind Deaf & Dumb Idiotic Disabled
South Side Magesterial District										
June 18, 1880										
Dwelling #168/Family #169										
William Wright	B	M	62			M		Blacksmith		
Martha Wright	B	F	42		Wife	M		Keeping House		
Willia A Wright	Mu	F	10		Daughter	S		at School		
Henry Hancock	B	M	14		Nephew	S		Works in Shop		
Enina Hancock	B	F	3		Neice	S				
Lissy Hancock	B	F	1		Neice	S				
Stonewall Dist										
June 2, 1880										
Dwelling #25/Family #26										
Wm W Wright	W	M	53			M		Farmer		1
Susan Wright	W	F	48		Wife	M		Keeping house		
Bettie Wright	W	F	21		Daughter	S		At Home		1
Joseph Wright	W	M	18		Son	S		Farm laborer		
James Wright	W	M	11		Son	S		Farm laborer		
Lucy Wright	W	F	8		Daughter	S				
Charles Wright	W	M	5		Son	S				
Mollie Childress	W	F	19		Daughter	M		At Home		
Dwelling #26/Family #27										
Wm F Wright	W	M	21			M		Farmer	2	
Blanche Wright	W	F	18		Wife	M		Keeping House		
Mollie Wright	W	F	11/12		Daughter	S				

Appendix: Appomattox County, Virginia, 1880 Census

Name continued from previous page]	Attended School Within Year	Cannot Read	Cannot Write	Born	Father Born	Mother Born	Identification
South Side Magesterial District June 18, 1880							
Dwelling #168/Family #169							
William Wright		1	1	Virginia	Va	Va	
Martha Wright		1	1	Virginia	Va	Va	
Willia A Wright	1			Virginia	Va	Va	
Henry Hancock		1	1	Virginia	Va	Va	
Enina Hancock				Virginia	Va	Va	
Lissy Hancock				Virginia	Va	Va	
Stonewall Dist June 2, 1880							
Dwelling #25/Family #26							
Wm W Wright		1	1	Virginia	Va	Va	William Wesley Wright
Susan Wright		1	1	Virginia	Va	Va	
Bettie Wright		1	1	Virginia	Va	Va	
Joseph Wright		1	1	Virginia	Va	Va	
James Wright		1	1	Virginia	Va	Va	
Lucy Wright				Virginia	Va	Va	
Charles Wright				Virginia	Va	Va	
Mollie Childress				Virginia	Va	Va	
Dwelling #26/Family #27							
Wm F Wright				Virginia	Va	Va	1923 William Fletcher Wright of Virginia, son of William Wesley
Blanche Wright				Virginia	Va	Va	Wright
Mollie Wright				Virginia	Va	Va	

Name	Color	Sex	Age	Month of Birth	Relationship	Marital Status	Married During Year	Occupation	Months Unemployed	Sickness Blind Deaf & Dumb Idiotic Disabled

June 3 & 4, 1880

Dwelling #59/Family #63

Name	Color	Sex	Age	Month of Birth	Relationship	Marital Status	Married During Year	Occupation	Months Unemployed	Sickness Blind Deaf & Dumb Idiotic Disabled
W W Wright	W	M	60			M		Farming		
Elizabeth Wright	W	F	45		wife	M		Keeping House		
Lelia Wright	W	F	18		Daughter	S		Daughter		
Mary H Wright	W	F	16		Daughter	S		At Home		
Madora Ann Wright	W	F	14		Daughter	S		At Home		
Bertha C Wright	W	F	12		Daughter	S		At Home		
Blanche Wright	W	F	11		Daughter	S		At Home		
Sam W Wright	W	M	7		Son	S				
Richard Wright	W	M	57		Brother	S		Laborer		

Dwelling #60/Family #64

Name	Color	Sex	Age	Month of Birth	Relationship	Marital Status	Married During Year	Occupation	Months Unemployed	Sickness Blind Deaf & Dumb Idiotic Disabled
Luther Wright	W	M	27			M		Farming		
Henrietta Wright	W	F	21		Wife	M		Keeping House		
Claude Wright	W	M	2		Son	S				
Lennie Wright	W	F	11/12		Daughter	S				

Appendix: Appomattox County, Virginia, 1880 Census

Name continued from previous page]	Attended School Within Year	Cannot Read	Cannot Write	Born	Father Born	Mother Born	Identification
June 3 & 4, 1880							
Dwelling #59/Family #63							
W W Wright				Virginia	Va	Va	William Washington Wright, son of 1881 William P. Wright of
Elizabeth Wright				Virginia	Va	Va	Appomattox County, grandson of Charles Wright, and great
Lelia Wright				Virginia	Va	Va	grandson of Robert Wright, Sr. (Campbell County)
Mary H Wright	1			Virginia	Va	Va	
Madora Ann Wright	1			Virginia	Va	Va	
Bertha C Wright	1			Virginia	Va	Va	
Blanche Wright				Virginia	Va	Va	
Sam W Wright				Virginia	Va	Va	
Richard Wright				Virginia	Va	Va	
Dwelling #60/Family #64							
Luther Wright				Virginia	Va	Va	1909 Luther Warren Wright of Lynchburg, son of 1880
Henrietta Wright				Virginia	Va	Va	Benjamin Edward Wright of Amherst County, grandson of 1881
Claude Wright				Virginia	Va	Va	William P. Wright of Appomattox County, great grandson of
Lennie Wright				Virginia	Va	Va	Charles Wright, and great great grandson of Robert Wright, Sr. (Campbell County) and Henrietta E. (Wright) Wright, daughter of 1891 Alexander Wright of Greenbrier County, West Virginia, granddaughter of Benjamin Wright of Amherst County, great granddaughter of 1830 Moses Wright of Amherst County, great great granddaughter of 1799 Benjamin Wright of Amherst County and great great great granddaughter of 1767 Francis Wright of Amherst County

Appendix: Appomattox County, Virginia, 1880 Census

Name	Color	Sex	Age	Monthof Birth	Relationship	Marital Status	Married During Year	Occupation	Months Unem- ployed	Sickness Blind Deaf & Dumb Idiotic Disabled

June 4 & 5, 1880

Dwelling #83/Family #87

Name	Color	Sex	Age	Monthof Birth	Relationship	Marital Status	Married During Year	Occupation	Months Unemployed	Sickness
Ann Wright	W	F	44					Domestic Servant		
Christopher Wright	W	M	20		Son			Laborer		
Cornelia Wright	W	F	21		Daughter	S		At Home		
Alice Wright	W	F	13		Daughter	S		At Home		
A P Johnson	W	M	78		Uncle	S		No occupation		
Luther Bernard	B	M	6		Servant	S				

June 9, 1880

Dwelling #164/Family #271

Name	Color	Sex	Age	Monthof Birth	Relationship	Marital Status	Married During Year	Occupation	Months Unemployed	Sickness
John Wright	W	M	28					Laborer		
Delia Wright	W	F	21		wife	M		Keeping House		
Wm Wright	W	M	10/12		Son	S				
Claude Howerton	B	M	6		Servant	S		Domestic Servant		
Robt Davis	B	M	21		Servant	S		Laborer		

June 11 & 12, 1880

Dwelling #212/Family #227

Name	Color	Sex	Age	Monthof Birth	Relationship	Marital Status	Married During Year	Occupation	Months Unemployed	Sickness
Jesse Wright	W	M	25			M		Carpenter		
Blanche Wright	W	F	21		wife	M		Keeping House		
Edwin Wright	W	M	2		son	S				

Appendix: Appomattox County, Virginia, 1880 Census

Name continued from previous page]	Attended School Within Year	Cannot Read	Cannot Write	Born	Father Born	Mother Born	Identification
June 4 & 5, 1880							
Dwelling #83/Family #87							
Ann Wright				Virginia	Va	Va	
Christopher Wright				Virginia	Va	Va	
Cornelia Wright				Virginia	Va	Va	
Alice Wright				Virginia	Va	Va	
A P Johnson				Virginia	Va	Va	
Luther Bernard				Virginia	Va	Va	
June 9, 1880							
Dwelling #164/Family #271							
John Wright				Virginia	Va	Va	1914 John W. Wright of Appomattox County, son of William Wesley Wright
Delia Wright				Virginia	Va	Va	
Wm Wright				Virginia	Va	Va	
Claude Howerton				Virginia	Va	Va	
Robt Davis				Virginia	Va	Va	
June 11 & 12, 1880							
Dwelling #212/Family #227							
Jesse Wright				Virginia	Va	Va	Jesse Hughes Wright, son of 1873 John Patterson Wright of Campbell County, grandson of 1811 John Wright of Campbell County, and great grandson of Robert Wright, Sr. (Campbell County)
Blanche Wright				Virginia	Va	Va	
Edwin Wright				Virginia	Va	Va	

Appendix: Appomattox County, Virginia, 1880 Census

Name	Color	Sex	Age	Monthof Birth	Relationship	Marital Status	Married During Year	Occupation	Months Unem- ployed	Sickness Blind Deaf & Dumb Idiotic Disabled

June 17, 1880

Dwelling #325/Family #343

Name	Color	Sex	Age	Monthof Birth	Relationship	Marital Status	Married During Year	Occupation	Months Unem- ployed	Sickness Blind Deaf & Dumb Idiotic Disabled
Sam Wright	W	M	30			M		Machinist		
Bettie Wright	W	F	24		wife	M		Keeping house		
Jesse Wright	W	M	6		Son	S				
Mary Wright	W	F	3		Daughter	S				
Bessie Wright	W	F	1		Daughter	S				
Fuller Drinkard	W	M	20		Boarder	S		At School		
Jno Drinkard	W	M	21		Boarder	S		Laborer		

Appendix: Appomattox County, Virginia, 1880 Census

Name continued from previous page]	Attended School Within Year	Cannot Read	Cannot Write	Born	Father Born	Mother Born	Identification
June 17, 1880							
Dwelling #325/Family #343							
Sam Wright				Virginia	Va	Va	Samuel Anderson Wright, son of 1873 John Patterson Wright of
Bettie Wright				Virginia	Va	Va	Campbell County, grandson of 1811 John Wright of Campbell
Jesse Wright				Virginia	Va	Va	County, and great grandson of Robert Wright, Sr. (Campbell
Mary Wright				Virginia	Va	Va	County)
Bessie Wright				Virginia	Va	Va	
Fuller Drinkard				Virginia	Va	Va	
Jno Drinkard				Virginia	Va	Va	

1900 CENSUS

APPOMATTOX COUNTY, VIRGINIA

Revised as of February 12, 2005

		Location			Relation			Personal Description							
In Cities		Number of dwelling houses in	Number of family in the	Name of each person whose place of	Relation-ship of each person				Date of Birth		Age at last birth-	Whether single, married, widowed, or	Number of years	Mother of how many	Number of these children
Street	House Number	the order of visitation	order of visitation	abode on June 1, 1900, was in this family.	to the head the family	Color or race	Sex	Month	Year	day	divorced	married	children	living

Clover Hill District June 5, 1900

		35	38	James Wright	Head	B	M	Nov	1841	58	M	30		
				Jane Wright	wife	B	F	Mar	1850	50	M	30	8	5
				William Wright	Son	B	M	Feb	1874	26	S			
				Brasco Wright	Son	B	M	Jun	1882	12	S			
				Magie Kelso	Sister	B	F	June	1871	28	wd		2	2
				Alsenia Kelso	Niece	B	F	June	1886	13	S			
				Earnest E Kelso	Nephew	B	M	Aug	1889	10	S			

Clover Hall District June 5, 1900

		50	54	Laura B Wright	Head	W	F	Aug	1861	38	Wd		5	5
				Cornelia Wright	Daughter	W	F	Dec	1885	14	S			
				Willie T. Wright	Son	W	M	May	1890	10	S			
				Joseph S. Wright	Son	W	M	Dec	1892	7	S			
				Robert L Wright	Son	W	M	May	1894	6	S			
				John A. Wright	Son	W	M	Aug	1896	4	S			

Name of each person whose place of abode on June 1, 1900, was in this family. [continued from prior page]	Nativity			Citizenship			Occupation, Trade, Or Profession of each person Ten Years of age and over.		Education			
	Place of birth of this Person	Place of birth of Father of this person	Place of birth of Mother of this person	Year of immi-gration to the United States	Number of years in the United States	Natural-ization	Occupation	Months not employed	Attended school in months)	Can read	Can write	Can speak English
James Wright	Virginia	Virginia	Virginia				Farmer	0		No	No	yes
Jane Wright	Virginia	Virginia	Virginia							No	No	yes
William Wright	Virginia	Virginia	Virginia				Farm Laborer	0		No	No	yes
Brasco Wright	Virginia	Virginia	Virginia				Farm Laborer	0		No	No	yes
Magie Kelso	Virginia	Virginia	Virginia				Farm Laborer	0		No	No	yes
Alsenia Kelso	Virginia	Virginia	Virginia						5	No	No	yes
Earnest E Kelso	Virginia	Virginia	Virginia						2	No	No	yes
Laura B Wright	Virginia	Virginia	Virginia				Farm Laborer	0		yes	yes	yes
Cornelia Wright	Virginia	Virginia	Virginia						2	yes	yes	yes
Willie T. Wright	Virginia	Virginia	Virginia				Farm Laborer	0		yes	yes	yes
Joseph S. Wright	Virginia	Virginia	Virginia						2			
Robert L Wright	Virginia	Virginia	Virginia						2			
John A. Wright	Virginia	Virginia	Virginia									

Name of each person whose place of abode on June 1, 1900, was in this family. [continued from prior page]	Ownership Of Home				Identification
	Owned or rented	Owned free or mortgaged	Farm or house	Number of farm schedule	
James Wright Jane Wright William Wright Brasco Wright Magie Kelso Alsenia Kelso Earnest E Kelso	R		F	33	
Laura B Wright Cornelia Wright Willie T. Wright Joseph S. Wright Robert L Wright John A. Wright	R		H		Laura Bell (Ferguson) Wright, widow of Christopher W. Wright, a son of Washington Wright

Appendix: Appomattox County, Virginia, 1900 Census

		Location			Relation			Personal Description							
		Number of dwelling houses in the order of	Number of family in the order of	Name of each person whose place of	Relation-ship of each person					Age at last birth-	Whether single, married, widowed,	Number of years	Mother of how many	Number of these children
In Cities	House			abode on June 1, 1900,	to the head	Color		Date of Birth			or			
Street	Number	visitation	visitation	was in this family.	the family	or race	Sex	Month	Year	day	divorced	married	children	living

Clover Hill District June 9, 1900

		124	126	John Wright	Head	W	M	July	1851	48	Wd			
				James W. Wright	Son	W	M	Aug	1878	21	S			
				Elizabeth S Wright	Daughter	W	F	Nov	1882	17				
				Rosa K Wright	Daughter	W	F	Sept	1885	14				
				Pattie M Wright	Daughter	W	F	Mar	1891	9				
				Jula Wright	Daughter	W	F	Apr	1894	6				
				Edgar C Wheeler	Laborer	W	M	May	1880	20	S			
				Frank Brady	laborer	W	M	Dec	1875	24	S			
				Susan Wright	Mother	W	F	Feb	1833	67	Wd		4	2

Clover Hill District June 28, 1900

		309	311	William Wright	Head	W	M	July	1857	42	M	22		
				Blanche N Wright	Wife	W	M	Jan	1862	38	M	22	1	1
				Berta N Wright	Daughter	W	F	June	1880	19	S			
				Lillie E. Wright	Daughter	W	F	July	1882	17	S			
				Thomas W Wright	Son	W	M	July	1886	13				
				Chessie C Wright	Daughter	W	F	June	1888	11				
				George W. Wright	Son	W	M	Mar	1891	9				
				Eddie A. Wright	Son	W	M	Mar	1893	7				
				Josie W Wright	Daughter	W	M	Jan	1896	4				
				Childress A Wright	Nephew	W	M	Apr	1888	12				
				Elisa L. Smith	Laborer	W	M	Oct	1864	25	Wd			

Name of each person whose place of abode on June 1, 1900, was in this family. [continued from prior page]	Nativity			Citizenship			Occupation, Trade, Or Profession of each person Ten Years of age and over.		Education			
	Place of birth of each person and parents of each person enumerated.			Year of immi-gration to the United States	Number of years in the United States	Natural-ization		Months not employed	Attended school in months)	Can read	Can write	Can speak English
	Place of birth of this Person	Place of birth of Father of this person	Place of birth of Mother of this person				Occupation					
John Wright	Virginia	Virginia	Virginia				Farmer	0				
James W. Wright	Virginia	Virginia	Virginia				Farm Laborer	4				
Elizabeth S Wright	Virginia	Virginia	Virginia									
Rosa K Wright	Virginia	Virginia	Virginia									
Pattie M Wright	Virginia	Virginia	Virginia									
Jula Wright	Virginia	Virginia	Virginia									
Edgar C Wheeler	Virginia	Virginia	Virginia				Farm laborer	0		yes	yes	yes
Frank Brady	Virginia	Germany	Ireland				Farm laborer	0		no	no	yes
Susan Wright	Virginia	Virginia	Virginia							yes	yes	yes
William Wright	Virginia	Virginia	Virginia				Farmer	0		yes	yes	yes
Blanche N Wright	Virginia	Virginia	Virginia							yes	yes	yes
Berta N Wright	Virginia	Virginia	Virginia						1	yes	yes	yes
Lillie E. Wright	Virginia	Virginia	Virginia				Farm laborer	1	1	yes	yes	yes
Thomas W Wright	Virginia	Virginia	Virginia				Farm laborer	1	1	yes	yes	yes
Chessie C Wright	Virginia	Virginia	Virginia									yes
George W. Wright	Virginia	Virginia	Virginia									yes
Eddie A. Wright	Virginia	Virginia	Virginia									yes
Josie W Wright	Virginia	Virginia	Virginia									
Childress A Wright	Virginia	Virginia	Virginia				Farm laborer	1	1	yes	yes	yes
Elisa L. Smith	Virginia	Virginia	Virginia				Farm laborer	0		yes	yes	yes

Appendix: Appomattox County, Virginia, 1900 Census

Name of each person whose place of abode on June 1, 1900, was in this family. [continued from prior page]	Ownership Of Home				Identification
	Owned or rented	Owned free or mortgaged	Farm or house	Number of farm schedule	
John Wright	R		F	63(?)	1914 John W. Wright of Appomattox County, son of William Wesley Wright
James W. Wright					
Elizabeth S Wright					
Rosa K Wright					
Pattie M Wright					
Jula Wright					
Edgar C Wheeler					
Frank Brady					
Susan Wright					
William Wright	R		F	226(?)	1923 William Fletcher Wright of Virginia, son of William Wesley Wright
Blanche N Wright					
Berta N Wright					
Lillie E. Wright					
Thomas W Wright					
Chessie C Wright					
George W. Wright					
Eddie A. Wright					
Josie W Wright					
Childress A Wright					
Elisa L. Smith					

Location				Relation										
In Cities		Number of dwelling houses in the order of	Number of family in the order of	Name of each person whose place of abode on June 1, 1900,	Relationship of each person to the head	Color			Date of Birth	Age at last birth-	Whether single, married, widowed, or	Number of years	Mother of how many	Number of these children
Street	House Number	visitation	visitation	was in this family.	the family	or race	Sex	Month	Year	day	divorced	married	children	living
Clover Hill District June 28, 1900														
		313	313	Washington Wright	Head	B	M	Sept	1852	47	M	20		
				Mildred Wright	Wife	B	F	May	1862	38	M	20	12	11
				James M Wright	Son	B	M	June	1884	16				
				Thomas E Wright	Son	B	M	May	1886	14				
				Ernest Wright	Son	B	M	June	1888	11				
				Frank W. Wright	Son	B	M	Dec	1889	10				
				Ada R Wright	Daughter	B	F	Feb	1891	9				
				Major S Wright	Son	B	M	Jun	1893	7				
				Mary M. Wright	Daughter	B	F	Oct	1895	5				
				Pitmund Wright	Son	B	M	Oct	1896	3				
				Yost Wright	Son	B	M	Sept	1898	1				
Clover Hill District June 28, 1900														
		315	317	Henry Wooldridge	Head	W	M	May	1848	52	M	15		
				Fannie B Wooldridge	Wife	W	F	Mar	1850	50	M	15	2	0
				Lucinda Wright	S in law	W	F	Apr	1845	55	S			

Appendix: Appomattox County, Virginia, 1900 Census

Name of each person whose place of abode on June 1, 1900, was in this family. [continued from prior page]	Nativity			Citizenship			Occupation, Trade, Or Profession of each person Ten Years of age and over.		Education			
	Place of birth of each person and parents of each person enumerated.			Year of immi-gration to the United States	Number of years in the United States	Natural-ization			Attended school in months)			Can speak English
	Place of birth of this Person	Place of birth of Father of this person	Place of birth of Mother of this person				Occupation	Months not employed		Can read	Can write	
Washington Wright	Virginia	Virginia	Virginia				Farmer	0		no	no	yes
Mildred Wright	Virginia	Virginia	Virginia							no	no	yes
James M Wright	Virginia	Virginia	Virginia				Farm Laborer	0		yes	yes	yes
Thomas E Wright	Virginia	Virginia	Virginia				Farm Laborer	0		no	no	yes
Ernest Wright	Virginia	Virginia	Virginia				Farm Laborer	0		no	no	yes
Frank W. Wright	Virginia	Virginia	Virginia									yes
Ada R Wright	Virginia	Virginia	Virginia									yes
Major S Wright	Virginia	Virginia	Virginia									yes
Mary M. Wright	Virginia	Virginia	Virginia									yes
Pittmund Wright	Virginia	Virginia	Virginia									
Yost Wright	Virginia	Virginia	Virginia									
Henry Wooldridge	Virginia	Virginia	Virginia				Farmer	1		yes	yes	yes
Fannie B Wooldridge	Virginia	Virginia	Virginia							yes	yes	yes
Lucinda Wright	Virginia	Virginia	Virginia							yes	yes	yes

Name of each person whose place of abode on June 1, 1900, was in this family. [continued from prior page]	Ownership Of Home				Identification
	Owned or rented	Owned free or mortgaged	Farm or house	Number of farm schedule	
Washington Wright Mildred Wright James M Wright Thomas E Wright Ernest Wright Frank W. Wright Ada R Wright Major S Wright Mary M. Wright Pittmund Wright Yost Wright	O	F	F	228	
Henry Wooldridge Fannie B Wooldridge Lucinda Wright	R		F	231	Lucinda P. Wright, daughter of 1882 Pryor B. Wright of Appomattox County, granddaughter of 1854 Samuel A. Wright of Appomattox County and granddaughter of 1815 Robert C. Wright of Prince Edward County, great granddaughter of 1820 Pryor Wright, Sr., of Prince Edward County, and great great granddaughter of 1779 John Wright of Prince Edward County

Appendix: Appomattox County, Virginia, 1900 Census

| | | | | | | | | Personal Description | | | | | | |
| | Location | | | | Relation | | | | | | | | | |

	In Cities		Number of dwelling houses in the order of visitation	Number of family in the order of visitation	Name of each person whose place of abode on June 1, 1900, was in this family.	Relation-ship of each person to the head the family	Color or race	Sex	Date of Birth Month	Year	Age at last birth-day	Whether single, married, widowed, or divorced	Number of years married	Mother of how many children	Number of these children living
Street	House Number														

Clover Hill District June 9, 1900

		323	325	Frank Gorge(?)	Head	W	M	Mar	1854	46	M	3		
				Susie J Gorge(?)	Wife	W	F	Apr	1870	30	M	3	1	1
				Marcie B Gorge(?)	Daughter	W	F	Dec	1899	6/12				
				Stewart J. Wright	Laborer	W	M	May	1887	13				

Southside Magisterial District June 19, 1900

		230	230	Taylor Wright	Head	B	M	Feb	1860	40	M	25		
				Lizza G Wright	Wife	B	F	Jan	1862	38	M	25	9	8
				Amherst Wright	Son	B	M	Aug	1884	15	S			
				_ed Wright	Son	B	M	Mar	1886	14	S			
				Laura Wright	Daughter	B	F	Apr	1888	12	S			
				Hallie B Wright	Son	B	M	Oct	1890	9	S			
				Ralph Wright	Son	B	M	Sep	1892	7	S			
				Charles E Wright	Son	B	M	Oct	1894	5	S			

Appendix: Appomattox County, Virginia, 1900 Census

Name of each person whose place of abode on June 1, 1900, was in this family. [continued from prior page]	Nativity Place of birth of each person and parents of each person enumerated.			Citizenship			Occupation, Trade, Or Profession of each person Ten Years of age and over.		Education			
	Place of birth of this Person	Place of birth of Father of this person	Place of birth of Mother of this person	Year of immi-gration to the United States	Number of years in the United States	Natural-ization	Occupation	Months not employed	Attended school in months)	Can read	Can write	Can speak English
Frank Gorge(?)	Virginia	Virginia	Virginia				Farmer	0		yes	yes	yes
Susie J Gorge(?)	Virginia	Virginia	Virginia							yes	yes	yes
Marcie B Gorge(?)	Virginia	Virginia	Virginia									
Stewart J. Wright	Virginia	Virginia	Virginia				Farm laborer	—		no	no	yes
Taylor Wright	Virginia	Virginia	Virginia				Farm labor			no	no	yes
Lizza G Wright	Virginia	Virginia	Virginia							no	no	yes
Amherst Wright	Virginia	Virginia	Virginia				Porter Hotel	0	0	yes	yes	yes
_ed Wright	Virginia	Virginia	Virginia				Farm Labor	0	0	yes	yes	yes
Laura Wright	Virginia	Virginia	Virginia				At School		5	yes	yes	yes
Hallie B Wright	Virginia	Virginia	Virginia				At School		5			
Ralph Wright	Virginia	Virginia	Virginia									
Charles E Wright	Virginia	Virginia	Virginia									

Name of each person whose place of abode on June 1, 1900, was in this family. [continued from prior page]	Ownership Of Home				Identification
	Owned or rented	Owned free or mortgaged	Farm or house	Number of farm schedule	
Frank Gorge(?) Susie J Gorge(?) Marcie B Gorge(?) Stewart J. Wright	O	F	F	238	
Taylor Wright Lizza G Wright Amherst Wright _ed Wright Laura Wright Hallie B Wright Ralph Wright Charles E Wright	R		H		

	Location				Relation		Personal Description								
In Cities Street	House Number	Number of dwelling houses in the order of visitation	Number of family in the order of visitation	Name of each person whose place of abode on June 1, 1900, was in this family.	Relation-ship of each person to the head the family	Color or race	Sex	Date of Birth Month	Year	Age at last birth-day	Whether single, married, widowed, or divorced	Number of years married	Mother of how many children	Number of these children living

Southside Magisterial District June 20, 1900

		247	247	Charles Wright	Head	B	M	Feb	1870	30	M	12		
				Emma Wright	Wife	B	F	Jan	1872	28	M	12	8	7
				George Wright	Son	B	M	Feb	1890	10	S			
				Nathaniel Wright	Son	B	M	May	1892	8	S			
				Collie Wright	Son	B	M	Sep	1892	7	S			
				Edith Wright	Daughter	B	F	May	1894	6	S			
				Alfred Wright	Son	B	M	Jan	1895	5	S			
				Gary Wright	Son	B	M	Sep	1897	2	S			
				Debbie(?) Sears	M in Law	B	F	Jan	1830	70	Wd		4	4
				Sue M Wright	Daughter	B	F	Feb	1885	15	S			
				Mary L McKinney	Niece	B	F	Feb	1900	3/12	S			

Southside Magisterial District June 20, 1900

		256	256	Henry Wright	Head	B	M	May	1851	49	Wd			
				Laura Wright	Son	B	M	Feb	1883	17	S			
				Lelia Wright	Daughter	B	F	Jan	1893	7	S			
				Anna M. Wright	Daughter	B	F	May	1895	5	S			
				Lizzie Wright	Daughter	B	F	Feb	1897	3	S			
				Bleny J Wright	Son	B	M	Jan	1898	2	S			
				Stephen Wright	Son	B	M	May	1891	9	S			
				Marriet(?) Folks	Lodger	B	F	Aug	1877	22	S			

Appendix: Appomattox County, Virginia, 1900 Census

Name of each person whose place of abode on June 1, 1900, was in this family. [continued from prior page]	Nativity			Citizenship			Occupation, Trade, Or Profession of each person Ten Years of age and over.		Education			
	Place of birth of each person and parents of each person enumerated.			Year of immi-gration to the United States	Number of years in the United States	Natural-ization						
	Place of birth of this Person	Place of birth of Father of this person	Place of birth of Mother of this person				Occupation	Months not employed	Attended school in months)	Can read	Can write	Can speak English
Charles Wright	Virginia	Virginia	Virginia				RR Laborer		0	yes	yes	yes
Emma Wright	Virginia	Virginia	Virginia							yes	yes	yes
George Wright	Virginia	Virginia	Virginia				At School		5	no	no	yes
Nathaniel Wright	Virginia	Virginia	Virginia						0			
Collie Wright	Virginia	Virginia	Virginia									
Edith Wright	Virginia	Virginia	Virginia									
Alfred Wright	Virginia	Virginia	Virginia									
Gary Wright	Virginia	Virginia	Virginia									
Debbie(?) Sears	Virginia	Virginia	Virginia							no	no	yes
Sue M Wright	Virginia	Virginia	Virginia						0	no	no	yes
Mary L McKinney	Virginia	Virginia	Virginia									
Henry Wright	Virginia	Virginia	Virginia				Farmer	0		No	No	yes
Laura Wright	Virginia	Virginia	Virginia				Farm labor	0	0	No	No	yes
Lelia Wright	Virginia	Virginia	Virginia									
Anna M. Wright	Virginia	Virginia	Virginia									
Lizzie Wright	Virginia	Virginia	Virginia									
Bleny J Wright	Virginia	Virginia	Virginia									
Stephen Wright	Virginia	Virginia	Virginia									
Marriet(?) Folks	Virginia	Virginia	Virginia				Servant	5		no	no	yes

Name of each person whose place of abode on June 1, 1900, was in this family. [continued from prior page]	Ownership Of Home				Identification
	Owned or rented	Owned free or mortgaged	Farm or house	Number of farm schedule	
Charles Wright	O	F	H		Charles H. Wright, son of Henry Wright
Emma Wright					
George Wright					
Nathaniel Wright					
Collie Wright					
Edith Wright					
Alfred Wright					
Gary Wright					
Debbie(?) Sears					
Sue M Wright					
Mary L McKinney					
Henry Wright	O	F	F	160	
Laura Wright					
Lelia Wright					
Anna M. Wright					
Lizzie Wright					
Bleny J Wright					
Stephen Wright					
Marriet(?) Folks					

Appendix: Appomattox County, Virginia, 1900 Census

Location					Relation			Personal Description						
In Cities		Number of dwelling houses in the order of visitation	Number of family in the order of visitation	Name of each person whose place of abode on June 1, 1900, was in this family.	Relationship of each person to the head the family	Color or race	Sex	Date of Birth		Age at last birthday	Whether single, married, widowed, or divorced	Number of years married	Mother of how many children	Number of these children living
Street	House Number							Month	Year					
Stonewall June __, 1900														
		116	122	Marth Wright	Head	W	F	Jan	1850	50	Wd		4	4
				Dellia Wright	Daughter	W	F	Mch	1875	25	S			
				Luther Wright	Son	W	M	Feb	1872	28	S			
				Laura Wright	Daughter	W	F	Apr	1880	20	S			
				Mildred Wright	Daughter	W	F	Jan	1881	8	S			
Stonewall District June 14, 1900														
		129	142	Wm W Wright	Head	W	M	Augt	1821	78	M	48		
				Elizabeth Wright	Wife	W	F	Jan	1836	64	M	48	10	7
				Richd T Wright	Brother	W	M	Mch	1823	77	S			
				Page H C Page	Son in Law	W	M	June	1854	45	M	10		
				Mary H Page	Daughter	W	F	Apl	1869	31	M	10	4	4
				Ruby S Page	Gr Daughter	W	F	Mch	1893	7	S			
				Mary E Page	Gr Daughter	W	F	Mch	1895	5				
				Alicia B Page	Gr Daughter	W	F	Dec	1896	3				
				Edward C Page	Gr Son	W	M	Apr	1899	1				

Appendix: Appomattox County, Virginia, 1900 Census

Name of each person whose place of abode on June 1, 1900, was in this family. [continued from prior page]	Nativity			Citizenship			Occupation, Trade, Or Profession of each person Ten Years of age and over.		Education			
	Place of birth of each person and parents of each person enumerated.			Year of immi-gration to the United States	Number of years in the United States	Natural-ization			Attended school in months)			
	Place of birth of this Person	Place of birth of Father of this person	Place of birth of Mother of this person				Occupation	Months not employed		Can read	Can write	Can speak English
Marth Wright	Virginia	Virginia	Virginia							yes	yes	yes
Dellia Wright	Virginia	Virginia	Virginia							yes	yes	yes
Luther Wright	Virginia	Virginia	Virginia				Farm Laborer			yes	yes	yes
Laura Wright	Virginia	Virginia	Virginia							yes	yes	yes
Mildred Wright	Virginia	Virginia	Virginia									
Wm W Wright	Virginia	Virginia	Virginia				Farmer			yes	yes	yes
Elizabeth Wright	Virginia	Virginia	Virginia							yes	yes	yes
Richd T Wright	Virginia	Virginia	Virginia				Day Laborer			no	no	yes
Page H C Page	Virginia	Virginia	Virginia				Farm Laborer			yes	yes	yes
Mary H Page	Virginia	Virginia	Virginia							yes	yes	yes
Ruby S Page	Virginia	Virginia	Virginia						0			
Mariah E Page	Virginia	Virginia	Virginia						0			
Alicia B Page	Virginia	Virginia	Virginia									
Edward C Page	Virginia	Virginia	Virginia									

Appendix: Appomattox County, Virginia, 1900 Census

Name of each person whose place of abode on June 1, 1900, was in this family. [continued from prior page]	Owned or rented	Owned free or mortgaged	Farm or house	Number of farm schedule	Identification
		Ownership Of Home			
Marth Wright			H		
Dellia Wright					
Luther Wright					
Laura Wright					
Mildred Wright					
Wm W Wright	O	F	F	72	William Washington Wright, son of 1881 William P. Wright of Appomattox County, grandson of Charles Wright, and great grandson of Robert Wright, Sr., (Campbell County)
Elizabeth Wright					
Richd T Wright					
Page H C Page					
Mary H Page					
Ruby S Page					
Mariah E Page					
Alicia B Page					
Edward C Page					

INDEX

Sears, Debbie, 58, 59, 60
Smith, Elisa L., 49, 50, 51
Smith, Martha, 13
Smith, Mary, 13
Turner, John L., 13
Turner, Mary E., 13
Turner, Mary S., 13
Turner, Rosa A., 13
Turner, Sarah E., 13
Wheeler, Edgar C, 49, 50, 51
Wooldridge, Fannie B, 52, 53
Wooldridge, Henry, 52, 53, 54
Wright, Ada R, 52, 53, 54
Wright, Adelia R., 2
Wright, Agie F, 30, 31
Wright, Alexander, 26, 27
Wright, Alfred, 58, 59, 60
Wright, Alice, 40, 41
Wright, Alice C., 20, 21
Wright, Amanda E., 2
Wright, Amherst, 55, 56, 57
Wright, Angeline A., 5
Wright, Ann, 18, 19, 40, 41
Wright, Ann C., 2, 20, 21
Wright, Anna M., 58, 59, 60
Wright, Arissa C., 4, 11
Wright, Aritha W., 16, 17
Wright, Augusta Anne, 26, 27
Wright, Barbary F., 4, 11
Wright, Barbary G., 8
Wright, Benjamin, 8, 18, 19, 30, 31
Wright, Benjamin E., 13
Wright, Benjamin W., 13
Wright, Beraregard, 30, 31
Wright, Berta N, 49, 50, 51
Wright, Bertha, 34, 35
Wright, Bertha C, 38, 39
Wright, Bessie, 42, 43

Wright, Bettie, 36, 37, 42, 43
Wright, Bettie S, 20, 21
Wright, Betty, 28, 29
Wright, Birelia A., 18, 19
Wright, Blanche, 36, 37, 38, 39, 40, 41
Wright, Blanche N, 49, 50, 51
Wright, Bleny J, 58, 59, 60
Wright, Bradford, 20, 21
Wright, Brasco, 46, 47, 48
Wright, Campbell C, 16, 17
Wright, Campbell S., 6, 10
Wright, Capella, 20, 21
Wright, Caroline W., 2
Wright, Casey B, 18, 19
Wright, Cassandale E., 5
Wright, Caswel, 16, 17
Wright, Caswell C., 4, 11
Wright, Catharine A., 5
Wright, Celia, 34, 35
Wright, Chambers L., 7
Wright, Charles, 18, 19, 36, 37, 58, 59, 60
Wright, Charles E, 55, 56, 57
Wright, Charles W., 13
Wright, Charlie, 34, 35
Wright, Chessie C, 49, 50, 51
Wright, Childress A, 49, 50, 51
Wright, Christopher, 20, 21, 40, 41
Wright, Christopher C., 2
Wright, Clara Belle, 28, 29
Wright, Claude, 38, 39
Wright, Claudius, 16, 17
Wright, Claudius F., 4
Wright, Claudius I., 10
Wright, Collie, 58, 59, 60
Wright, Columbus H., 7
Wright, Cornelia, 20, 21, 40, 41, 46, 47, 48
Wright, Cornelius, 20, 21
Wright, Cornelius A., 4

Wright, Cornelius C., 11
Wright, Crosby, 8
Wright, Cuzzy, 7
Wright, Cynthia A., 6
Wright, Daniel P., 6
Wright, David, 34, 35
Wright, David M., 14
Wright, Davy, 18, 19
Wright, Delia, 40, 41
Wright, Dellia, 61, 62, 63
Wright, Dooda, 28, 29
Wright, Dora Ann, 22, 23
Wright, Eddie A., 49, 50, 51
Wright, Edith, 58, 59, 60
Wright, Edwin, 40, 41
Wright, Elisa Jane, 26, 27
Wright, Elisabeth, 26, 27
Wright, Elizabeth, 5, 6, 8, 22, 23, 38, 39, 61, 62, 63
Wright, Elizabeth F., 4
Wright, Elizabeth I., 14
Wright, Elizabeth S, 12, 49, 50, 51
Wright, Emilia A., 2
Wright, Emilia M., 2
Wright, Emma, 58, 59, 60
Wright, Ernest, 52, 53, 54
Wright, Euclid, 7
Wright, F. B., 34, 35
Wright, Fannie, 16, 17
Wright, Fielding A., 13
Wright, Fountain C., 7
Wright, Frances, 8
Wright, Frank, 22, 23
Wright, Frank W., 52, 53, 54
Wright, Gary, 58, 59, 60
Wright, Geo. W., 4
Wright, George, 26, 27, 58, 59, 60
Wright, George A., 4

Wright, George G., 18, 19
Wright, George W., 49, 50, 51
Wright, George W. A., 11
Wright, Gilliam, 7
Wright, Hallie B, 55, 56, 57
Wright, Harris C., 6
Wright, Harry, 34, 35
Wright, Hattie, 20, 21
Wright, Henrietta, 38, 39
Wright, Henry, 18, 19, 22, 23, 26, 27, 34, 35, 58, 59, 60
Wright, Henry D., 6
Wright, James, 20, 21, 30, 31, 36, 37, 46, 47, 48
Wright, James A., 3, 12
Wright, James D., 5
Wright, James M, 52, 53, 54
Wright, James R, 20, 21
Wright, James S., 3
Wright, James W., 49, 50, 51
Wright, Jane, 3, 7, 28, 29, 46, 47, 48
Wright, Jemima, 11
Wright, Jesse, 40, 41, 42, 43
Wright, Jim, 28, 29
Wright, John, 40, 41, 49, 50, 51
Wright, John A., 46, 47, 48
Wright, John D., 6
Wright, John J., 8
Wright, John W, 12, 13, 20, 21
Wright, Joseph, 36, 37
Wright, Joseph S., 46, 47, 48
Wright, Josie W, 49, 50, 51
Wright, Judith, 3
Wright, Jula, 49, 50, 51
Wright, Kezziah, 7
Wright, Kiziah B., 11
Wright, Laura, 55, 56, 57, 58, 59, 60, 61, 62, 63
Wright, Laura B, 46, 47, 48
Wright, Leanirs J., 7

Wright, Lelia, 38, 39 58, 59, 60
Wright, Lelice F, 22
Wright, Lennie, 38, 39
Wright, Lillie E., 49, 50, 51
Wright, Lilly F, 30, 31
Wright, Lizza G, 55, 56, 57
Wright, Lizzie, 34, 35, 58, 59, 60
Wright, Loving A., 8, 11
Wright, Lucinda, 34, 35, 52, 53, 54
Wright, Lucinda P., 4, 11, 16, 17
Wright, Lucy, 36, 37
Wright, Lucy J., 3
Wright, Luther, 38, 39, 61, 62, 63
Wright, Luther W., 13
Wright, Madora Ann, 38, 39
Wright, Major S, 52, 53, 54
Wright, Malissa A., 7
Wright, Marey, 28, 29
Wright, Maria L., 20, 21, 26, 27
Wright, Mariah, 12
Wright, Mariah J., 6, 10
Wright, Mariettie, 30, 31
Wright, Marriah, 7
Wright, Marth, 61, 62, 63
Wright, Martha, 8, 10, 16, 17, 36, 37
Wright, Martha C., 22
Wright, Martha J., 2
Wright, Martha L., 11
Wright, Martine, 26, 27
Wright, Mary, 12, 18, 19, 32, 33, 34, 35, 42, 43
Wright, Mary A., 4, 6
Wright, Mary Anne, 26, 27
Wright, Mary E., 2
Wright, Mary F., 7, 12, 13
Wright, Mary H, 22, 23, 38, 39
Wright, Mary J., 3, 4, 11, 16, 17
Wright, Mary M., 52, 53, 54
Wright, Mary S., 8

Wright, Melinda, 30, 31
Wright, Mildred, 52, 53, 54, 61, 62, 63
Wright, Mildred A., 6, 10, 16, 17
Wright, Mollie, 36, 37
Wright, Molly, 30, 31
Wright, Nancy, 12, 16, 17
Wright, Nancy B., 16, 17
Wright, Nancy C., 4, 10, 11
Wright, Nancy J., 5
Wright, Nathaniel, 58, 59, 60
Wright, Ovid B., 7
Wright, Pattie M, 49, 50, 51
Wright, Philis, 22, 23
Wright, Phoebe, 13
Wright, Pitmund, 52, 53, 54
Wright, Pryer B, 34, 35
Wright, Pryor, 7
Wright, Pryor B., 4, 11, 16, 17
Wright, Ralph, 55, 56, 57
Wright, Reubin, 18, 19
Wright, Richard, 38, 39
Wright, Richard H., 22
Wright, Richard T., 3, 14
Wright, Richd T, 61, 62, 63
Wright, Robert, 5, 6
Wright, Robert B., 7, 14, 22, 23
Wright, Robert J., 7
Wright, Robert L, 46, 47, 48
Wright, Robert P., 4
Wright, Robt P., 11
Wright, Rosa K, 49, 50, 51
Wright, S L, 32, 33
Wright, Sam, 30, 31, 42, 43
Wright, Sam W, 38, 39
Wright, Saml A., 11
Wright, Samuel A., 8
Wright, Samuel T., 3
Wright, Sarah B., 22, 23

Wright, Sarah E, 20, 21
Wright, Sarah J., 12
Wright, Saunders, 16, 17
Wright, Saunders F., 4, 11
Wright, Silia F., 14
Wright, Stephen, 58, 59, 60
Wright, Stewart J., 55, 56, 57
Wright, Sue M, 58, 59, 60
Wright, Susan, 18, 19, 34, 35, 36, 37, 49, 50, 51
Wright, Susan F., 12
Wright, Taylor, 20, 21, 55, 56, 57
Wright, Thomas, 6, 16, 17
Wright, Thomas E, 52, 53, 54
Wright, Thomas H., 10, 12
Wright, Thomas O. P., 2
Wright, Thomas P., 2
Wright, Thomas S., 8
Wright, Thomas W., 2, 49, 50, 51
Wright, Victoria, 18, 19, 34, 35
Wright, Virginia A., 10
Wright, W W, 38, 39
Wright, Washington, 22, 23, 52, 53, 54
Wright, Willia A, 36, 37
Wright, William, 5, 7, 18, 19, 20, 21, 22, 36, 37,
  46, 47, 48, 49, 50, 51
Wright, William A., 8
Wright, William Henry, 26, 27
Wright, William M., 8
Wright, William P., 3, 6
Wright, William R., 2
Wright, William W., 3
Wright, Willie, 34, 35
Wright, Willie A., 10
Wright, Willie T., 46, 47, 48
Wright, Willis, 16, 17, 28, 29
Wright, Wilson M., 5
Wright, Wm, 40, 41
Wright, Wm F, 36, 37

Wright, Wm W., 22, 23, 36, 37, 61, 62, 63
Wright, Wm. F., 12
Wright, Wm. P., 13
Wright, Wm. W., 12, 14
Wright, York, 18, 19, 26, 27
Wright, York N, 18, 19
Wright, Yost, 52, 53, 54

0128(032506)

WRIGHT FAMILY

DEED RECORDS

APPOMATTOX COUNTY, VIRGINIA

1845 to 1910

Revised as of November 3, 2005

This document is an appendix to a larger work titled <u>Sorting Some Of The Wrights Of Southern Virginia</u>. The work is divided into parts for each family of Wrights that has been researched. Each part is divided into two sections; the first section is text discussing the family and the evidence supporting the relationships and the second section is a descendants chart summarizing the relationships and information known about each individual.

The appendices to the work (of which this document is one) present source records for persons named Wright by county and by type of record with the identification of the person named and their Wright ancestors to the extent known.

The source for the records listed in this appendix is the following:

> 1) Appomattox County, Virginia, Index of Deeds and Deeds, available from the Clerk of the Circuit Court, P.O. Box 672, Appomattox, Virginia 24522.

The identification of a person or their ancestor by year and county indicates their year of death and county of residence at death. For example, "1763 Thomas Wright of Bedford County" indicates that this was the Thomas Wright who died in 1763 in Bedford County. If no state is listed after the county, the state is Virginia; counties in states other than Virginia will have a state listed after the county, as in "1876 William S. Wright of Highland County, Ohio".

A parenthetical after the name indicates an identification of the person when a place of death is not yet known, as in "John Wright (Goochland County Carpenter)". A county in parentheses after the name indicates the county with which that person was most identified when no evidence of the place of death has yet been found, as in "Grief Wright (Bedford County)".

All or portions of the text and descendants charts for each Wright family identified are available from the author:

> Robert N. Grant
> 15 Campo Bello Court   (H) 650-854-0895
> Menlo Park, California 94025   (O) 650-614-3800

This is a work in progress and I would be most interested in receiving additional information about any of the persons identified in these records in order to correct any errors or expand on the information given.

Appendix: Appomattox County, Virginia, Deed Records

Book/Page	Date	Grantor	Grantee	Instrument	Identification
					Court records before 1892 were burned
10 467	1852/04/21	Preston B. Stone	Daniel P Wright	Option	Daniel P. Wright, son of 1811 John Wright of Campbell County and grandson of Robert Wright, Sr., (Campbell County)
02 112	1872/12/17	Pryor Wright Est by Comr	N. H. Ragland	Deed	Estate of 1854 Pryor Rucker Wright, Jr., of Appomattox County, son of 1820 Pryor Wright, Sr., of Prince Edward County and grandson of 1779 John Wright of Prince Edward County
04 033	1884/01/25	Saunders F. Wright & Virginia A. Wright	Hartwell H. Scruggs	Deed	Saunders F. Wright, son of 1882 Pryor B. Wright of Appomattox County, grandson of 1854 Samuel A. Wright of Appomattox County, great grandson of 1820 Pryor Wright, Sr., of Prince Edward County and great great grandson of 1779 John Wright of Prince Edward County
04 338	1886/04/05	Wm W. Wright	John J Carson, Tr.	Deed of Trust	William Washington Wright, son of 1881 William P. Wright of Appomattox County, grandson of Charles Wright, and great grandson of Robert Wright, Sr., (Campbell County)
02 508	1889/11/13	Saunders F. Wright	Sam'l M. Bryan	Deed & Plat	Saunders F. Wright, son of 1882 Pryor B. Wright of Appomattox County, grandson of 1854 Samuel A. Wright of Appomattox County, great grandson of 1820 Pryor Wright, Sr., of Prince Edward County and great great grandson of 1779 John Wright of Prince Edward County
01 238	1893/03/24	Washington Wright & Mildred Wright	Robert C. Harvey, Tr.	Deed of Trust	
01 551	1894/03/19	Saunders F. Wright	Mary J. Wooldridge & Fanny Wooldridge & Lucinda P. Wright	Deed	Grantor: Saunders F. Wright, son of 1882 Pryor B. Wright, of Appomattox County, grandson of 1854 Samuel A. Wright of Appomattox County, great grandson of 1820 Pryor Wright, Sr., of Prince Edward County and great great grandson of 1779 John Wright of Prince Edward County Grantees: Sisters of Saunders F. Wright

Appendix: Appomattox County, Virginia, Deed Records

Book/Page	Date	Grantor	Grantee	Instrument	Identification
02 320	1894/04/28	John C. Ferguson	Laura B. Wright	Deed	Laura Bell (Ferguson) Wright, widow of Christopher W. Wright, a son of Washington Wright
03 237	1896/10/08	Judith Christian & Isham Christian & Mary Walker	Henry M. Wright	Deed & Plat	
06 147	1901/03/01	Jennie E McKinney	Luther W Wright	Bond	Luther William Wright, son of Ann C. (____) Wright
07 198	1902/11/04	Chas. H Wright & Emma Wright	J. R. Horsley Tr.	Deed of Trust	Charles H. Wright, son of Henry Wright
07 043	1903/02/09	Jennie E McKinney	Luther W Wright	Deed	Luther William Wright, son of Ann C. (____) Wright
07 094	1903/04/28	J L Foster & Bessie M Foster	W. F. Wright	Deed	1923 William Fletcher Wright of Virginia, son of William Wesley Wright
07 095	1903/04/28	W. F. Wright & Blanch Wright	J. R. Atwood, Tr.	Deed of Trust	1923 William Fletcher Wright of Virginia, son of William Wesley Wright
07 358	1904/05/03	Saunders F. Wright & Agnes E. Wright	Fannie B. Wooldridge	Deed	Grantor: Saunders F. Wright, son of 1882 Pryor B. Wright of Appomattox County, grandson of 1854 Samuel A. Wright of Appomattox County, great grandson of 1820 Pryor Wright, Sr., of Prince Edward County, and great great grandson of 1779 John Wright of Prince Edward County Grantee: Fannie B. (Wright) Wooldridge, daughter of 1882 Pryor B. Wright of Appomattox County, granddaughter of 1854 Samuel A. Wright of Appomattox County, great granddaughter of 1820 Pryor Wright of Prince Edward County, and great great granddaughter of 1779 John Wright of Prince Edward County
07 335	1904/05/19	Wm W Wright	Elizabeth S Wright	Deed	William Washington Wright, son of 1881 William P. Wright of Appomattox County, grandson of Charles Wright, and probably great grandson of Robert Wright, Sr., (Campbell County)

Appendix: Appomattox County, Virginia, Deed Records

Book/Page	Date	Grantor	Grantee	Instrument	Identification
07 433	1904/11/28	Nelson Elam by Comm	Eliza Wright	Deed	
08 166	1905/10/04	L. W. Wright & Mary A. Wright	S. L. Ferguson, Tr.	Deed of Trust	Luther William Wright, son of Ann C. (____) Wright
08 175	1905/10/25	Henry Anderson & M E Anderson	Thomas H Wright	Deed	
08 176	1905/10/25	Saml E Anderson & B W Anderson	Thomas H Wright	Deed	
09 135	1906/03/09	James W. Flood & Lizzie Flood	Lillie Conner Wright	Plat	
08 421	1906/04/18	L. W. Wright & Mary A. Wright	T. W. Moses	Deed	Luther William Wright, son of Ann C. (____) Wright
09 085	1906/12/18	Taylor Wright & Eliza Wright	S. L. Ferguson, Tr.	Deed of Trust	
09 093	1906/12/21	Thomas Sears	R. C. Wright	Deed	
09 094	1906/12/21	R. C. Wright	W. F. Wright, Tr.	Deed of Trust	
09 095	1907/01/01	Ann R. Durrum	Chas H. Wright	Deed	Charles H. Wright, son of Henry Wright
09 096	1907/01/01	Chas. H Wright & Emma Wright	S. L. Ferguson, Tr.	Deed of Trust	Charles H. Wright, son of Henry Wright
09 431	1907/11/23	Pryor Wright Sr., Est. by Nannie C. Williams and John C. Williams	William Rosser	Deed	Grantor: Nannie C. or J. (Wright) Williams, daughter of Campbell S. Wright, granddaughter of 1854 Pryor Rucker Wright, Jr., of Appomattox County, great granddaughter of 1820 Pryor Wright, Sr., of Prince Edward County, and great great granddaughter of 1779 John Wright of Prince Edward County

Appendix: Appomattox County, Virginia, Deed Records

Book/Page	Date	Grantor	Grantee	Instrument	Identification
10 375	1909/01/19	Charles H. Wright & Emma Wright	J. R. Horseley Tr.	Deed of Trust	Charles H. Wright, son of Henry Wright
10 526	1909/03/07	Wilber Stratton & M S Wilber	Thomas H Wright	Deed	
11 315	1909/11/12	J. R. Horsley, Special Commissioner for the estate of York Wright	S. L. Ferguson	Deed	
11 402	1910/01/15	Chas. H. Wright & Emma Wright	J. R. Horsley, Tr.	Deed of Trust	Charles H. Wright, son of Henry Wright
11 531	1910/02/10	William L. Phillips & Ann Phillips	J. A. Wright	Deed	
12 010	1910/04/25	John J Carson & W. C. Page, and G. W. Stanley, Trustees	W. W. Wright heirs	Release of Deed of Trust	Estate of William Washington Wright, son of 1881 William P. Wright of Appomattox County, grandson of Charles Wright, and probably great grandson of Robert Wright, Sr., (Campbell County)
12 012	1910/05/05	Elizabeth S. Wright	A. A. Bell	Deed	Elizabeth S. (____) Wright, widow of William Washington Wright, a son of 1881 William P. Wright of Appomattox County, grandson of Charles Wright, and great grandson of Robert Wright, Sr., (Campbell County)
12 386	1910/06/07	Helena Wright Est	J. R. Horsley	Deed & Plat	Helena (____) Wright, wife of 1881 William P. Wright of Appomattox County, a son of Charles Wright, and probably grandson of Robert Wright, Sr., (Campbell County)

INDEX

Appendix: Appomattox County, Virginia, Deed Records

Book/Page	Date	Grantor	Grantee	Instrument	Identification
2 242	1911/01/14	J. A. Wright & Mattie I. Wright	J. C. Bishop	Deed	
12 316	1911/03/06	Wm A. Dixon _	E F Wright	Deed	
12 317	1911/03/06	E. F Wright & Mary E. Wright	S. L. Ferguson, Tr.	Deed of Trust	
12 431	1911/05/23	Annie Wright & Saml H. Wright	Martha C. Lane	Deed	
12 539	1911/08/30	Roberta W Harvey	R. H. Wright	Deed	
12 571	1911/09/30	Chas. H Wright & Emma Wright	L. F. Ferguson, Tr.	Deed of Trust	Charles H. Wright, son of Henry Wright
13 065	1912/01/18	Wm. M. Wright	Chas H. Diuguid	Deed	
13 104	1912/02/17	E. F Wright & Mary E. Wright	J. M Riddle	Deed	
13 177	1912/03/27	Chas. H Wright & Emma Wright	D. L. Ferguson	Deed	Charles H. Wright, son of Henry Wright
14 586	1912/08/28	Walter Wright & Armanda Wright	L. F. Ferguson Tr.	Deed of Trust	
13 492	1912/09/03	R. H. Wright & Ethel L. Wright	C. H. Sackett & H M Sackett	Deed of Trust	
15 172	1914/03/02	Geo A Christian & Mary Christian	Chas Wright	Deed	
15 173	1914/03/02	Chas. H Wright & Emma Wright	D. L Ferguson Tr.	Deed of Trust	Charles H. Wright, son of Henry Wright

Appendix: Appomattox County, Virginia, Deed Records

Book/Page	Date	Grantor	Grantee	Instrument	Identification
15 223	1914/04/07	E. F. Wright	J. M. Riddle	Release	
15 480	1914/11/17	J. A. Wright	S. L. Ferguson, Tr.	Deed of Trust	
15 479	1914/11/17	John C. Ferguson & M L Ferguson	W. T. Wright	Deed	
15 479	1914/11/17	John C Ferguson & M L Ferguson	J. A. Wright	Deed	
15 480	1914/11/17	W. T. Wright & Annie B. Wright	S. L. Ferguson, Tr.	Deed of Trust	
15 559	1915/02/02	Walter A. Wright & Mildred Wright	Fred'k Wright	Deed	
15 559	1915/02/02	W A Wright & Amanda Wright	Fredk C Wright	Deed	
16 106	1915/05/15	Chas. H Wright & Emma Wright	L. F. Ferguson	Deed	Charles H. Wright, son of Henry Wright
16 126	1915/05/27	Nanny A Fuqua by Exor	E. Cammie Wright	Deed	
16 565	1916/07/29	John A. Wright	J. S. Wright & W. T. Wright	Deed	

WRIGHT FAMILY

LAND TAX LISTS

APPOMATTOX COUNTY, VIRGINIA

1845 to 1863

Revised as of January 27, 2006

Introduction To Appendix: Land Tax Lists for Appomattox County, Virginia

This document is an appendix to a larger work titled Sorting Some Of The Wrights Of Southern Virginia. The work is divided into parts for each family of Wrights that has been researched. Each part is divided into two sections; the first section is text discussing the family and the evidence supporting the relationships and the second section is a descendants chart summarizing the relationships and information known about each individual.

The appendices to the work (of which this document is one) present source records for persons named Wright by county and by type of record with the identification of the person named and their Wright ancestors to the extent known.

The source for the records listed in this appendix is the following:

1) Appomattox County, Virginia, Land Tax Lists, available from The Virginia State Library And Archives, 11th & Capitol Streets, Richmond, Virginia 23219-3491.

The identification of a person or their ancestor by year and county indicates their year of death and county of residence at death. For example, "1763 Thomas Wright of Bedford County" indicates that this was the Thomas Wright who died in 1763 in Bedford County. If no state is listed after the county, the state is Virginia; counties in states other than Virginia will have a state listed after the county, as in "1876 William S. Wright of Highland County, Ohio".

A parenthetical after the name indicates an identification of the person when a place of death is not yet known, as in "John Wright (Goochland County Carpenter)". A county in parentheses after the name indicates the county with which that person was most identified when no evidence of the place of death has yet been found, as in "Grief Wright (Bedford County)".

All or portions of the text and descendants charts for each Wright family identified are available from the author:

Robert N. Grant
15 Campo Bello Court   (H) 650-854-0895
Menlo Park, California 94025   (O) 650-614-3800

This is a work in progress and I would be most interested in receiving additional information about any of the persons identified in these records in order to correct any errors or expand on the information given.

1318(012706)

1845 LAND TAX LIST

APPOMATTOX COUNTY, VIRGINIA

Appendix: Appomattox County, Virginia, 1845 Land Tax List:

Persons transferred from Buckingham District:

Name Of Owner	Residence	Estate whether held in Fee simple, life &c	No. of Acres	Description of the land, as to watercourses, mountains and contiguous tracts	Distance and bearing from the courthouse	Value of land per acre, including buildings	Sum added to the land on account of buildings	Total value of the land and buildings
Helena Wright			100	W Wreck Island	29 W	7.00	100.00	700.00
John M Wright			140	on W David's Cr	20 SW	3.00		420.00

Appendix: Appomattox County, Virginia, 1845 Land Tax List:

Persons transferred from Buckingham District:

Name Of Owner [Continued from prior page]	Am't of tax on on the whole tract, at the legal rate	Explanation of altera- tions during the pre- ceding year, especially from whom transferred	Identification
Helena Wright	.70		Helena (____) Wright, wife of 1881 William P. Wright of Appomattox County, a son of Charles Wright and grandson of Robert Wright, Sr. (Campbell County
John M Wright	.42	from Dr Wm D Christian &c	

Appendix: Appomattox County, Virginia, 1845 Land Tax List:

Persons transferred from Campbell County:

Name Of Owner	Residence	Estate whether held in fee simple, life &c	No. of Acres	Description of the land, as to watercourses, mountains and contiguous tracts	Distance and bearing from the courthouse	Value of land per acre, including buildings	Sum added to the land on account of buildings	Total value of the land and buildings
John P. Wright	Appomattox	Fee	67½	Wreck Island		4.00	100.00	270.00
Pryor Wright	Appomattox	Fee	25	Falling River	15	6.00		150.00
W. M. Wright	Appomattox	Fee	12	Cub Creek	20 E	3.00	36.00	250.00
George A Wright	Appomattox	Fee	10-1/8	Stone Wall	15.00	4.00		40.50

Appendix: Appomattox County, Virginia, 1845 Land Tax List:

Persons transferred from Campbell County:

Name Of Owner [Continued from prior page]	Am't of tax on on the whole tract, at the legal rate	Explanation of alterations during the preceding year, especially from whom transferred	Identification
John P. Wright	.27		1873 John Patterson Wright of Campbell County, son of 1811 John Wright of Campbell County and grandson of Robert Wright, Sr. (Campbell County)
Pryor Wright	.15		1854 Pryor Rucker Wright, Jr., of Appomattox County, son of 1820 Pryor Wright, Sr., of Prince Edward County and grandson of 1779 John Wright of Prince Edward County
W. M. Wright	.04		1897 William M. Wright of Bedford County, son of 1854 Samuel A. Wright of Appomattox County, grandson of 1820 Pryor Wright, Sr., of Prince Edward County, and great grandson of 1779 John Wright of Prince Edward County
George A Wright	.04		1879 George Anderson Wright of Campbell County, son of 1811 John Wright of Campbell County and grandson of Robert Wright, Sr. (Campbell County)

Appendix: Appomattox County, Virginia, 1845 Land Tax List:

Persons transferred from Charlotte County:

Name Of Owner	Residence	Estate whether held in fee simple, life &c	No. of Acres	Description of the land, as to watercourses, mountains and contiguous tracts	Distance and bearing from the courthouse	Value of land per acre, including buildings	Sum added to the land on account of buildings	Total value of the land and buildings
[No Wrights listed]								

Appendix: Appomattox County, Virginia, 1845 Land Tax List:

Persons transferred from Charlotte County:

Name Of Owner [Continued from prior page]	Am't of tax on on the whole tract, at the legal rate	Explanation of alterations during the preceding year, especially from whom transferred	Identification

[No Wrights listed]

Appendix: Appomattox County, Virginia, 1845 Land Tax List:

Persons transferred from Prince Edward County:

Name Of Owner	Residence	Estate whether held in fee simple, life &c	No. of Acres	Description of the land, as to watercourses, mountains and contiguous tracts	Distance and bearing from the courthouse	Value of land per acre, including buildings	Sum added to the land on account of buildings	Total value of the land and buildings
Pryor Wright senr.			144	Hugh Rain	30	10.00	100.00	1440.00
Robert C Wright Esta			79-1/3	John Sears	30 NW	8.50	100.00	674.33
Thomas Wright Esta			127	Hugh Rain		5.00		635.00
Samuel Wright	Buckingham	Trust	171-1/5	John Morriss	15	4.50		770.44

Appendix: Appomattox County, Virginia, 1845 Land Tax List:

Persons transferred from Prince Edward County:

Name Of Owner [Continued from prior page]	Am't of tax on on the whole tract, at the legal rate	Explanation of alterations during the preceding year, especially from whom transferred	Identification
Pryor Wright senr.	1.44		1854 Pryor Rucker Wright, Jr., of Appomattox County, son of 1820 Pryor Wright, Sr., of Prince Edward County and grandson of 1779 John Wright of Prince Edward County
Robert C Wright Esta	.68		Estate of 1815 Robert C. Wright of Prince Edward County, son of 1820 Pryor Wright, Sr., of Prince Edward County and grandson of 1779 John Wright of Prince Edward County
Thomas Wright Esta	.64		Estate of 1842 Thomas Wright of Prince Edward County, son of 1820 Pryor Wright, Sr., of Prince Edward County and grandson of 1779 John Wright of Prince Edward County
Samuel Wright	.77	From John Morris 1842	

1318(012706)

1846 LAND TAX LIST

APPOMATTOX COUNTY, VIRGINIA

Appendix: Appomattox County, Virginia, 1845 Land Tax List:

Thomas W John District:

Name Of Owner	Residence	Estate whether held in Fee simple, life &c	No. of Acres	Description of the land, as to watercourses, mountains and contiguous tracts	Distance and bearing from the courthouse	Value of land per acre, includ-ing buildings	Sum added to the land on account of buildings	Total value of the land and buildings
Helena Wright	Resident	Fee	100	Wreck Island	10 NW	7.00	100.00	700.00
John M Wright	Resident	Fee	140	David's Creek	7 NE	3.00		420.00
John P Wright	Resident	Fee	67-1/2	Wreck Island	10 NW	4.00	200.00	270.00
Pryor Wright Sr	Resident	Fee	25	Falling River	6 SW	6.00		150.00
Wm M. Wright	Resident	Fee	12	Cub Creek	10 S	3.00		36.00
George A Wright	Resident	Fee	10-1/8	Stone Wall	12 NW	4.50		40.50
Do	"	"	47-1/4	Same	12 NW	4.00	400.00	189.00
Robert C. Wright Est	Resident	Fee	73-1/3	adj Jno. Sears	1 W	8.50	100.00	674.33
Thomas Wright Est	Resident	Fee	127	adj Hugh Rain	1 W	5.00		635.00
Samuel Wright	Buckingham	Trust	171-1/5	adj John Morriss	15 E	4.50		770.40

Appendix: Appomattox County, Virginia, 1846 Land Tax List:

Thomas W John District:

Name Of Owner [Continued from prior page]	Am't of tax on on the whole tract, at the legal rate	Explanation of altera- tions during the pre- ceding year, especially from whom transferred	Identification
Helena Wright	.70		Helena (_____) Wright, wife of 1881 William P. Wright of Appomattox County, a son of Charles Wright, and grandson of Robert Wright, Sr. (Campbell County)
John M Wright	.42		
John P Wright	.27		1873 John Patterson Wright of Campbell County, son of 1811 John Wright of Campbell County and grandson of Robert Wright, Sr. (Campbell County)
Pryor Wright Sr	.15		1854 Pryor Rucker Wright, Jr., of Appomattox County, son of 1820 Pryor Wright, Sr., of Prince Edward County and grandson of 1779 John Wright of Prince Edward County
Wm M. Wright	.04		1897 William M. Wright of Bedford County, son of 1854 Samuel A. Wright of Appomattox County, grandson of 1820 Pryor Wright, Sr., of Prince Edward County, and great grandson of 1779 John Wright of Prince Edward County
George A Wright	.04		1879 George Anderson Wright of Campbell County, son of 1811 John Wright of Campbell
Do	.19		County and grandson of 1779 John Wright of Prince Edward County
Robert C. Wright Est	.68		Estate of 1815 Robert C. Wright of Prince Edward County, son of 1820 Pryor Wright, Sr., of Prince Edward County and grandson of Robert Wright, Sr. (Campbell County)
Thomas Wright Est	.64		Estate of 1842 Thomas Wright of Prince Edward County, son of 1820 Pryor Wright, Sr., of Prince Edward County and grandson of 1779 John Wright of Prince Edward County
Samuel Wright	.77		

1847 LAND TAX LIST

APPOMATTOX COUNTY, VIRGINIA

Appendix: Appomattox County, Virginia, 1847 Land Tax List:

Thomas W John District:

Name Of Owner	Residence	Estate whether held in Fee simple, life &c	No. of Acres	Description of the land, as to watercourses, mountains and contiguous tracts	Distance and bearing from the courthouse	Value of land per acre, includ-ing buildings	Sum added to the land on account of buildings	Total value of the land and buildings
Helena Wright	Resident	Fee	100	Wreck Island	_ NW	7.00	100.00	700.00
John M Wright	Resident	Fee	140	Davids Creek	_ NE	3.00		420.00
John P Wright	Resident	Fee	67-1/2	Wreck Island	_ NW	4.00	100.00	270.00
Pryor Wright Sr	Resident	Fee	144	adj S D McDearman	_ S	10.00	100.00	1440.00
Do			15-1/4	adj Wm Patteson	_ SE	1.00		15.25
Wm M. Wright	Resident	Fee	12	Cub Creek	_ S	3.00		36.00
George A Wright	Resident	Fee	10-1/8	Stone Wall	_ NW	4.00		4.50
Do	"	"	47-1/4	Same	_ NW	4.00	100.00	189.00
Ro. C. Wright Est	Resident	Fee	73-1/3	adj Jno. Searl	_ E	4.47		894.00
Thomas Wright Est	Resident	Fee	127	adj Saml D McDermon	_ W	8.50	100.00	674.33
Saml Wright	Buckingham	Trust	171-1/5	adj Jno Morriss	_ E	6.00	100.00	412.50

Appendix: Appomattox County, Virginia, 1847 Land Tax List:

Thomas W John District:

Name Of Owner [Continued from prior page]	Am't of tax on on the whole tract, at the legal rate	Explanation of alterations during the preceding year, especially from whom transferred	Identification
Helena Wright	.70		Helena (____) Wright, wife of 1881 William P. Wright of Appomattox County, a son of Charles Wright, and grandson of Robert Wright, Sr. (Campbell County)
John M Wright	.42		
John P Wright	.27		1873 John Patterson Wright of Campbell County, son of 1811 John Wright of Campbell County and grandson of Robert Wright, Sr. (Campbell County)
Pryor Wright Sr Do	1.44 .02		1854 Pryor Rucker Wright, Jr., of Appomattox County, son of 1820 Pryor Wright, Sr., of Prince Edward Countyr Rucker Wright, Jr., of Appomattox County and grandson of 1779 John Wright of Prince Edward County
Wm M. Wright	.04		1897 William M. Wright of Bedford County, son of 1854 Samuel A. Wright of Appomattox County, grandson of 1820 Pryor Wright, Sr., of Prince Edward County, and great grandson of 1779 John Wright of Prince Edward County
George A Wright Do	.04 .19		1879 George Anderson Wright of Campbell County, son of 1811 John Wright of Campbell County and grandson of Robert Wright, Sr. (Campbell County)
Ro. C. Wright Est	.68		Estate of 1815 Robert C. Wright of Prince Edward County, son of 1820 Pryor Wright, Sr., of Prince Edward County and grandson of 1779 John Wright of Prince Edward County
Thomas Wright Est	.64		Estate of 1842 Thomas Wright of Prince Edward County, son of 1820 Pryor Wright, Sr., of Prince Edward County and grandson of 1779 John Wright of Prince Edward County
Saml Wright	.42		

1318(012706)

1848 LAND TAX LIST

APPOMATTOX COUNTY, VIRGINIA

Appendix: Appomatox County, Virginia, 1848 Land Tax List:

Thomas W John District:

Name Of Owner	Residence	Estate whether held in Fee simple, life &c	No. of Acres	Description of the land, as to watercourses, mountains and contiguous tracts	Distance and bearing from the courthouse	Value of land per acre, including buildings	Sum added to the land on account of buildings	Total value of the land and buildings
Helena Wright	Resident	fee	100	Wreck Island	_ NW	7.00	100.00	700.00
John M Wright	Resident	fee	140	Davids Creek	_ NE	3.00		420.00
John P Wright	Resident	fee	67-1/2	Wreck Island	_ NW	4.50	100.00	270.00
Pryor Wright Senr	Resident	fee	144	adj Saml McDearman	_ S	10.00	100.00	1440.00
do			15-1/4	adj William Patteson	_ SE	1.00		15.75
William M Wright	Resident	fee	12	Cub Creek	_ SE	3.00		36.00
George A Wright	Resident	fee	10-1/8	Stone Wall	_ NW	4.00		40.50
do	"	"	47-1/4	Same	_ NW	7.20	250.00	330.00
Robert C. Wright Estate	Resident	fee	73-1/3	adj John James	_ W	5.00		635.00
Thomas Wright Estate	Resident	fee	127	adj Sam P McDearman	_ E	7.00	650.00	2319.87
Samuel Wright	Buckingham	fee	171-1/5	adj John Morris	_ E	7.47		2793.78

Appendix: Appomatox County, Virginia, 1848 Land Tax List:

Thomas W John District:

Name Of Owner [Continued from prior page]	Am't of tax on the whole tract, at the legal rate	Explanation of alter- ations during the pre- ceding year, especially from whom transferred	Identification
Helena Wright	.70		Helena (____) Wright, wife of 1881 William P. Wright of Appomattox County, a son of Charles Wright, and grandson of Robert Wright, Sr. (Campbell County)
John M Wright	.42		
John P Wright	.27		1873 John Patterson Wright of Campbell County, son of 1811 John Wright of Campbell County and grandson of Robert Wright, Sr. (Campbell County)
Pryor Wright Senr	1.44		1854 Pryor Rucker Wright, Jr., of Appomattox County, son of 1820 Pryor Wright, Sr., of
do	.02		Prince Edward County and grandson of 1779 John Wright of Prince Edward County
Wm M. Wright	.04		1897 William M. Wright of Bedford County, son of 1854 Samuel A. Wright of Appomattox County, grandson of 1820 Pryor Wright, Sr., of Prince Edward County, and great grandson of 1779 John Wright of Prince Edward County
George A Wright	.04		1879 George Anderson Wright of Campbell County, son of 1811 John Wright of Campbell
do	.33	150 added for new buildings	County and grandson of Robert Wright, Sr. (Campbell County)
Robert C. Wright Estate	.64		Estate of 1815 Robert C. Wright of Prince Edward County, son of 1820 Pryor Wright, Sr., of Prince Edward County and grandson of 1779 John Wright of Prince Edward County
Thomas Wright Estate	2.32		Estate of 1842 Thomas Wright of Prince Edward County, son of 1820 Pryor Wright, Sr., of Prince Edward County and grandson of 1779 John Wright of Prince Edward County
Samuel Wright	7.80		

Appendix: Appomatox County, Virginia, 1848 Land Tax List:

Town Lots:

Name Of Owner	Residence	Kind of Estate	of Lot	Name of the Town	_ of Buildings	Value of lots including Buildings	Yearly Rent	Amt of Tax on lots at the __ _____	Identification
Pryor Wright	part of two lots	fee	32 P 26 Quantity not stated						

1849 LAND TAX LIST

APPOMATTOX COUNTY, VIRGINIA

Appendix: Appomattox County, Virginia, 1849 Land Tax List:

Thomas W John District:

Name Of Owner	Residence	Estate whether held in Fee simple, life &c	No. of Acres	Description of the land, as to watercourses, mountains and contiguous tracts	Distance and bearing from the courthouse	Value of land per acre, including buildings	Sum added to the land on account of buildings	Total value of the land and buildings
Helena Wright	Resident	in fee	100	Wreck Island	10 NW	7.00	100.00	700.00
John M Wright	Resident	in fee	140	Davids Creek	7 NE	3.00		420.00
John P Wright	Resident	in fee	67-1/2	Wreck Island	10 NW	4.50	100.00	270.00
Pryor Wright Senr	Resident	in fee	144	adj Saml M Dearman	1/2 S	10.00	100.00	1440.00
"			15-1/4	adj Wm Patteson	3 S	1.00		15.25
William M Wright	Resident	in fee	12	Cub Creek	10 SE	3.00		36.00
George A Wright	Resident	in fee	10-1/8	Stone Wall	12 NW	4.00		40.50
"	"	"	47-1/4	"	12 NW	7.20	250.00	330.00
Robert C. Wright Estate	Resident	in fee	73-1/3	adj John James	1 W	8.50	100.00	674.33
Thomas Wright Estate	Resident	in fee	127	adj Sam D McDearman	1 W	5.00		635.00
Samuel Wright	Buckingham	in fee	171-1/5	adj John Morris	15 E	4.50		770.40

Appendix: Appomattox County, Virginia, 1849 Land Tax List:

Thomas W John District:

Name Of Owner [Continued from prior page]	Am't of tax on the whole tract, at the legal rate	Explanation of alterations during the preceding year, especially from whom transferred	Identification
Helena Wright	.70		Helena (____) Wright, wife of 1881 William P. Wright of Appomattox County, a son of Charles Wright, and grandson of Robert Wright, Sr. (Campbell County)
John M Wright	.42		
John P Wright	.27		1873 John Patterson Wright of Campbell County, son of 1811 John Wright of Campbell County and grandson of Robert Wright, Sr. (Campbell County)
Pryor Wright Senr	1.44	Wm C Wooldridge land to Jef(?) Furbush	1854 Pryor Rucker Wright, Jr., of Appomattox County, son of 1820 Pryor Wright, Sr., of Prince Edward County and grandson of 1779 John Wright of Prince Edward County
do	.02		
Wm M. Wright	.04		1897 William M. Wright of Bedford County, son of 1854 Samuel A. Wright of Appomattox County, grandson of 1820 Pryor Wright, Sr., of Prince Edward County, and great grandson of 1779 John Wright of Prince Edward County
George A Wright	.04		1879 George Anderson Wright of Campbell County, son of 1811 John Wright of Campbell County and grandson of Robert Wright, Sr. (Campbell County)
"	.33		
Robert C. Wright Estate	.68		Estate of 1815 Robert C. Wright of Prince Edward County, son of 1820 Pryor Wright, Sr., of Prince Edward County and grandson of 1779 John Wright of Prince Edward County
Thomas Wright Estate	.64		Estate of 1842 Thomas Wright of Prince Edward County, son of 1820 Pryor Wright, Sr., of Prince Edward County and grandson of 1779 John Wright of Prince Edward County
Samuel Wright	.77		

1850 LAND TAX LIST

APPOMATTOX COUNTY, VIRGINIA

Appendix: Appomattox County, Virginia, 1850 Land Tax List:

Thomas W John District:

Name Of Owner	Residence	Estate whether held in Fee simple, life &c	No. of Acres	Description of the land, as to water-courses, mountains and contiguous tracts	Distance and bearing from the courthouse	Value of land per acre, including buildings	Sum added to the land on account of buildings	Total value of the land and buildings
Helena Wright	Resident	fee	100	Wreck Island	10 NW	7.00	100.00	700.00
John M Wright	Resident	fee	140	Davids Creek	7 NE	3.00		420.00
"	"	"	10	"	7 NE	5.00		50.00
John P Wright	Resident	fee	67-1/2	Wreck Island	10 NW	4.50	100.00	270.00
Pryor Wright Senr	Resident	fee	144	adj Saml McDearman	1/2 S	10.00	100.00	1440.00
"	"	fee	15-1/4	adj Wm Patteson Estate	3 SE	1.00		15.75
"	"	fee	30	adj Mc Dearman	1/2 W	10.00		500.00
William M Wright	Resident	fee	12	Cub Creek	10 SE	3.00		36.00
George A Wright	Resident	fee	10-1/8	Stone Wall	12 NW	4.00		40.50
"	"	fee	47-1/4	"	12 NW	7.20	250.00	330.00
Robert C. Wright Estate	Resident	fee	73-1/3	adj John Sears(?)	1 W	8.50	100.00	674.33
Samuel Wright	Buckingham	fee	171-1/5	adj John Morris	15 E	4.50		770.40
Samuel A Wright Lot No 3	Resident	fee	86-1/2	adj Lot No 7 near Eleanor Hill	1 W	6.00		519.00

Appendix: Appomattox County, Virginia, 1850 Land Tax List:

<u>Thomas W John District</u>:

Name Of Owner [Continued from prior page]	Am't of tax on the whole tract, at the legal rate	Explanation of alter- ations during the pre- ceding year, especially from whom transferred	Identification
Helena Wright	.70		Helena (____) Wright, wife of 2822 William P. Wright of Appomatox County, a son of Charles Wright, and grandson of Robert Wright, Sr. (Campbell County)
John M Wright	.42		
"	.05	From Geo. W. Johnson	
John P Wright	.27		1873 John Patterson Wright of Campbell County, son of 1811 John Wright of Campbell County and grandson of Robert Wright, Sr. (Campbell County)
Pryor Wright Senr	1.44		1854 Pryor Rucker Wright, Jr., of Appomattox County, son of 1820 Pryor Wright, Sr., of Prince Edward County and grandson of 1779 John Wright of Prince Edward County
"	.02		
"	.50	fr Thos Wrights land	
Wm M. Wright	.04		1897 William M. Wright of Bedford County, son of 1854 Samuel A. Wright of Appomattox County, grandson of 1820 Pryor Wright, Sr., of Prince Edward County, and great grandson of 1779 John Wright of Prince Edward County
George A Wright	.04		1879 George Anderson Wright of Campbell County, son of 1811 John Wright of Campbell County and grandson of Robert Wright, Sr. (Campbell County)
"	.33		
Robert C. Wright Estate	.68		Estate of 1815 Robert C. Wright of Prince Edward County, son of 1820 Pryor Wright, Sr., of Prince Edward County and grandson of 1779 John Wright of Prince Edward County
Samuel Wright	.77		
Samuel A Wright Lot No 3	.52	part Thos Wrights land	1854 Samuel A. Wright of Appomattox County, son of 1820 Pryor Wright, Sr., of Prince Edward County and grandson of 1779 John Wright of Prince Edward County

Appendix: Appomatox County, Virginia, 1850 Land Tax List:

Town Lots:

Name Of Owner	Residence	Estate whether in fee simple for life &c	Number of each lot in the town	Name of Town	Value of buildings	Value of lots including buildings	Yearly rent of lots	Amt of Tax on lots at the legal rate	Identification
Pryor Wright of 24 & 32	qty not stated	fee		Clover Hill	600.00	610.00		.61	1854 Pryor Rucker Wright, Jr., of Appomattox County, son of 1820 Pryor Wright, Sr., of Prince Edward County, and grandson of 1779 John Wright of Prince Edward County

1851 LAND TAX LIST

APPOMATTOX COUNTY, VIRGINIA

Appendix: Appomattox County, Virginia, 1851 Land Tax List:

Jonathan Christian District:

Name Of Owner	Residence	Estate whether held in Fee simple, life &c	No. of Acres	Description of the land, as to watercourses, mountains and contiguous tracts	Distance and bearing from the courthouse	Value of land per acre, including buildings	Sum added to the land on account of buildings	Total value of the land and buildings
Helena Wright	Resident	life	100	On Wreck Island	10 NW	6.00	100.00	600.00
John P Wright	Resident	Fee	69-1/2	On Wreck Island	10 NW	4.50		303.75
Pryor Wright	Resident	Fee	144	adj S D McDearman	1/2 S	15.00	300.00	2160.00
"	"	Fee	15-1/2	adj Wm Pattesons Est	5 SE	2.00		30.50
"	"	Fee	50	adj McDearman	1/2 W	10.00		500.00
William M Wright	Resident	Fee	12	on Prince Edward Road	10 SE	53.00	80.00	120.00
George A Wright	Resident	Fee	10-1/8	Stone Wall	12 NW	4.00		40.50
"	"	Fee	47-1/4	"	12 NW	7.00	150.00	330.75
Robert C Wright Est	Resident	Fee	73-1/3	adj John Sears(?)	1 W	8.50	100.00	674.33
Samuel Wright	Buckingham	Fee	171-1/5	adj John Morris	15 E	5.00	200.00	855.62
Samuel A Wright	Resident	Fee	86-1/2	Near Clover Hill	1 W	10.00		865.00

Appendix: Appomattox County, Virginia, 1851 Land Tax List:

Jonathan Christian District:

Name Of Owner [Continued from prior page]	Am't of tax on the whole tract, at the legal rate	Explanation of alter- ations during the pre- ceding year, especially from whom transferred	Identification
Helena Wright	.72		Helena (_____) Wright, wife of 1881 William P. Wright of Appomattox County, a son of Charles Wright, and grandson of Robert Wright, Sr. (Campbell County)
John P Wright	.37		1873 John Patterson Wright of Campbell County, son of 1811 John Wright of Campbell County and grandson of Robert Wright, Sr. (Campbell County)
Pryor Wright Senr " "	2.59 .04 .60		1854 Pryor Rucker Wright, Jr., of Appomattox County, son of 1820 Pryor Wright, Sr., of Prince Edward County and grandson of 1779 John Wright of Prince Edward County
Wm M. Wright	.15		1897 William M. Wright of Bedford County, son of 1854 Samuel A. Wright of Appomattox County, grandson of 1820 Pryor Wright, Sr., of Prince Edward County, and great grandson of 1779 John Wright of Prince Edward County
George A Wright "	.05 .40		1879 George Anderson Wright of Campbell County, son of 1811 John Wright of Campbell County and grandson of Robert Wright, Sr. (Campbell County)
Robert C Wright Est	.81		Estate of 1815 Robert C. Wright of Prince Edward County, son of 1820 Pryor Wright, Sr., of Prince Edward County and grandson of 1779 John Wright of Prince Edward County
Samuel Wright	1.03		
Samuel A Wright	1.04		1854 Samuel A. Wright of Appomattox County, son of 1820 Pryor Wright, Sr., of Prince Edward County and grandson of 1779 John Wright of Prince Edward County

1852 LAND TAX LIST

APPOMATTOX COUNTY, VIRGINIA

Appendix: Appomattox County, Virginia, 1852 Land Tax List:

Jonathan Christian District:

Name Of Owner	Residence	Estate whether held in Fee simple, life &c	No. of Acres	Name of Tract	Description of the land, as to watercourses, mountains and contiguous tracts	Distance and bearing from the courthouse	Value of land per acre, including buildings	Sum added to the land on account of buildings	Total value of the land and buildings
Helena Wright	Resident	Life	100		On Wreck Island	10 NW	6.00	100.00	532.00
John P Wright	Resident	Fee	69-1/2		On Wreck Island	10 NW	4.50		303.75
Pryor Wright Senr	Resident	Fee	144		Adj S D McDearman	1/2 S	15.00	300.00	2160.00
"	"	"	15-1/2		Adj W. Pattersons Est	5 SE	2.00		31.00
"	"	"	80		Adj McDearman	1/2 W	10.00		500.00
William M Wright	Resident	Fee	12		Adj P Edward Road	3 SW	10.00	80.00	120.00
George A Wright	Resident	Fee	10-1/8		Stone Wall	12 NW	4.00		40.50
"	"	"	47-1/2		"	12 NW	7.00	150.00	330.75
R C Wright Estate	Resident	Fee	73-1/3		Adj John Sears	1 W	8.50	100.00	674.33
Samuel Wright	Buckingham	Fee	171-1/8		Adj Jno Means	15 E	5.00	200.00	855.62
Samuel A Wright	Resident	Fee	Lot No 3 86-1/2		Near Clover Hill	1 W	10.00		865.00

Appendix: Appomattox County, Virginia, 1852 Land Tax List:

Jonathan Christian District:

Name Of Owner [Continued from prior page]	Amount of tax on the whole tract, at the legal rate	Amount of tax for county purposes	Explanation of alterations during the preceding year, especially from whom transferred	Identification
Helena Wright	1.08			Helena (_____) Wright, wife of 1881 William P. Wright of Appomattox County, a son of Charles Wright, and grandson of Robert Wright, Sr. (Campbell County)
John P Wright	.54			1873 John Patterson Wright of Campbell County, son of 1811 John Wright of Campbell County and grandson of Robert Wright, Sr. (Campbell County)
Pryor Wright Senr " "	3.89 .05 .90			1854 Pryor Rucker Wright, Jr., of Appomattox County, son of 1820 Pryor Wright, Sr., of Prince Edward County and grandson of 1779 John Wright of Prince Edward County
William M Wright	.40			1897 William M. Wright of Bedford County, son of 1854 Samuel A. Wright of Appomattox County, grandson of 1820 Pryor Wright, Sr., of Prince Edward County, and great grandson of 1779 John Wright of Prince Edward County
George A Wright "	.47 .60			1879 George Anderson Wright of Campbell County, son of 1811 John Wright of Campbell County and grandson of Robert Wright, Sr. (Campbell County)
R C Wright Estate	1.21			Estate of 1815 Robert C. Wright of Prince Edward County, son of 1820 Pryor Wright, Sr., of Prince Edward County and grandson of 1779 John Wright of Prince Edward County
Samuel Wright	1.54			
Samuel A Wright	1.56			1854 Samuel A. Wright of Appomattox County, son of 1820 Pryor Wright, Sr., of Prince Edward County and grandson of 1779 John Wright of Prince Edward County

1853 LAND TAX LIST

APPOMATTOX COUNTY, VIRGINIA

Appendix: Appomattox County, Virginia, 1853 Land Tax List:

Jonathan Christian District:

Name Of Owner	Residence	Estate whether held in Fee simple, life &c	No. of Acres	Name of Tract	Description of the land, as to water-courses, mountains and contiguous tracts	Distance and bearing from the courthouse	Value of land per acre, including buildings	Sum added to the land on account of buildings	Total value of the land and buildings
Helana Wright	Resident	Life	100		on Wreck Island	10 NW	6.00	100.00	600.00
John P Wright	Resident	Fee	69-1/2		On Wreck Island	10 NW	4.50		343.75
Pryor Wright Sen	Resident	Fee	144		Adj S D McDearman	1/2 W	15.00	300.00	2160.00
"	"	"	15-1/2		Adj Wm. Patterson Est	5 SE	2.00		31.00
"	"	"	50		Adj S D McDearman	1/2 W	10.00		500.00
William M Wright	Resident	Fee	12		On Prince Edward Road	3 SW	10.00	80.00	120.00
Robert C Wright Est	Resident	Fee	73-1/3		Adj John Sears	1 W	8.50	100.00	674.33
Samuel Wright	Buckingham	Fee	171-1/8		Adj John Morris	15 E	5.00	200.00	855.62
Samuel A Wright Lot 3	Resident	Fee	86-1/2		Adj Lot 2 near Clover Hill	1 W	10.00		865.00

Appendix: Appomattox County, Virginia, 1853 Land Tax List:

Jonathan Christian District:

Name Of Owner [Continued from prior page]	Amount of tax on the whole tract, at the legal rate	Amount of tax for county purposes	Explanation of alter- ations during the pre- ceding year, especially from whom transferred	Identification
Helana Wright	1.20			Helena (____) Wright, wife of 1881 William P. Wright of Appomattox County, a son of Charles Wright, and grandson of Robert Wright, Sr. (Campbell County)
John P Wright	.61			1873 John Patterson Wright of Campbell County, son of 1811 John Wright of Campbell County and grandson of Robert Wright, Sr. (Campbell County)
Pryor Wright Senr " "	4.32 .06 1.00			1854 Pryor Rucker Wright, Jr., of Appomattox County, son of 1820 Pryor Wright, Sr., of Prince Edward County and grandson of 1779 John Wright of Prince Edward County
William M Wright	.24			1897 William M. Wright of Bedford County, son of 1854 Samuel A. Wright of Appomattox County, grandson of 1820 Pryor Wright, Sr., of Prince Edward County, and great grandson of 1779 John Wright of Prince Edward County
Robert C Wright Est	1.35			Estate of 1815 Robert C. Wright of Prince Edward County, son of 1820 Pryor Wright, Sr., of Prince Edward County and grandson of 1779 John Wright of Prince Edward County
Samuel Wright	1.71			
Samuel A Wright	1.73			1854 Samuel A. Wright of Appomattox County, son of 1820 Pryor Wright, Sr., of Prince Edward County and grandson of 1779 John Wright of Prince Edward County

Appendix: Appomattox County, Virginia, 1853 Land Tax List:

Town Lots in District of Isaac Adam:

Name Of Owner	Residence	Estate whether in fee simple for life &c	Number of each lot in the town or a description of the part of lot owned	Name of Town	Value of buildings	Value of lots including buildings	Amount of tax on lots at the legal rate	Amount of tax for county purposes
Pryor Wright	Resident	Fee	Lot 24 & 32	Clover Hill	500.00	600.00	1.20	

Appendix: Appomatox County, Virginia, 1853 Land Tax List:

Town Lots in District of Isaac Adam:

Name Of Owner [Continued from prior page]	Explanation of alterations during the preceding year especially from whom transferred, and how the owner derived the property	Identification
Pryor Wright		1854 Pryor Rucker Wright, Jr., of Appomattox County, son of 1820 Pryor Wright, Sr., of Prince Edward County and grandson of 1779 John Wright of Prince Edward County

1854 LAND TAX LIST

APPOMATTOX COUNTY, VIRGINIA

Appendix: Appomattox County, Virginia, 1854 Land Tax List:

<u>Isaac Adam District</u>:

Name Of Owner	Residence	Estate whether held in Fee simple, life &c	No. of Acres	Name of Tract	Description of the land, as to watercourses, mountains and contiguous tracts	Distance and bearing from the courthouse	Value of land per acre, including buildings	Sum added to the land on account of buildings	Total value of the land and buildings
Helania Wright	Resident	Life	100		on Wreck Island	10 NW	6.00	100.00	600.00
John P Wright	Resident	Fee	69-1/2		On Wreck Island	10 NW	4.50		343.75
Pryor Wright Sen	Resident	Fee	144		Adj S D McDearman	1/2 W	15.00	300.00	2160.00
"	"	"	15-1/2		Adj W Patterson Est	5 SE	2.00		31.00
"	"	"	50		Adj S D McDearman	1/2 W	10.00		500.00
William M Wright	Resident	Fee	12		On Prince Edward Island	3 SW	10.00	80.00	120.00
Robert C Wright Est	Resident	Fee	73-1/3		Adj John Sears	1 W	8.50	100.00	623.33
Samuel Wright	Buckingham	Fee	171-1/8		Adj Jno Morris	15 E	5.00	200.00	855.62
Wm M Wright & Chs H Duiguid	Resident	Fee	1/2		Adj Clover Hill	15 NW	100.00	50.00	50.00
Samuel T. Wright	Resident	Fee	10		on Appomattox	1 W	8.25	50.00	87.50

Appendix: Appomattox County, Virginia, 1854 Land Tax List:

<u>Isaac Adam District</u>:

Name Of Owner [Continued from prior page]	Amount of tax on the whole tract, at the legal rate	Amount of tax for county purposes	Explanation of alterations during the preceding year, especially from whom transferred	Identification
Helania Wright	1.20			Helena (____) Wright, wife of 1881 William P. Wright of Appomattox County, a son of Charles Wright, and grandson of Robert Wright, Sr. (Campbell County)
John P Wright	.61			1873 John Patterson Wright of Campbell County, son of 1811 John Wright of Campbell County and grandson of Robert Wright, Sr. (Campbell County)
Pryor Wright Senr " "	4.32 .06 1.00			1854 Pryor Rucker Wright, Jr., of Appomattox County, son of 1820 Pryor Wright, Sr., of Prince Edward County and grandson of 1779 John Wright of Prince Edward County
William M Wright	.24		____ to Jos A Wood_	1897 William M. Wright of Bedford County, son of 1854 Samuel A. Wright of Appomattox County, grandson of 1820 Pryor Wright, Sr., of Prince Edward County, and great grandson of 1779 John Wright of Prince Edward County
Robert C Wright Est	1.25			Estate of 1815 Robert C. Wright of Prince Edward County, son of 1820 Pryor Wright, Sr., of Prince Edward County and grandson of 1779 John Wright of Prince Edward County
Samuel Wright	1.71			
Wm M Wright & Chs H Duiguid	.10		From S D McDearman & wife	
Samuel T. Wright	.17		From S D McDearman & wife	Samuel T. Wright, son of 1854 Samuel A. Wright of Appomattox County, grandson of 1820 Pryor Wright, Sr., of Prince Edward County, and great grandson of 1779 John Wright of Prince Edward County

Appendix: Appomattox County, Virginia, 1854 Land Tax List:

Town Lots in District of Isaac Adam:

Name Of Owner	Residence	Estate whether in fee simple for life &c	Number of each lot in the town or a description of the part of lot owned	Name of Town	Value of buildings	Value of lots including buildings	Amount of tax on lots at the legal rate	Amount of tax for county purposes
Pryor Wright	Resident	Fee	part of 24 & 32	Clover Hill	500.00	600.00	1.20	

Appendix: Appomattox County, Virginia, 1854 Land Tax List:

Name Of Owner [Continued from prior page]	Explanation of alterations during the preceding year especially from whom transferred, and how the owner derived the property	Identification
Pryor Wright		1854 Pryor Rucker Wright, Jr., of Appomattox County, son of 1820 Pryor Wright, Sr., of Prince Edward County and grandson of 1779 John Wright of Prince Edward County

1855 LAND TAX LIST

APPOMATTOX COUNTY, VIRGINIA

Appendix: Appomattox County, Virginia, 1855 Land Tax List:

Isaac Adam District:

Name Of Owner	Residence	Estate whether held in Fee simple, life &c	No. of Acres	Name of Tract	Description of the land, as to watercourses, mountains and contiguous tracts	Distance and bearing from the courthouse	Value of land per acre, including buildings	Sum added to the land on account if buildings	Total value of the land and buildings
Helena Wright	Resident	Life	100		on Wreck Island	10 NW	6.00	100.00	600.00
John P Wright	Lynchburg	Fee	69-1/2		On Wreck Island	10 NW	4.50		343.75
Pryor Wright Sen Est	Resident	Fee	144		Adj S D McDearman	1/2 W	15.00	300.00	2450.00
"	"	"	15-1/2		Adj W Patterson Est	5 SE	2.00		
"	"	"	50		Adj S D McDearman	1/2 W	10.00		500.00
Parker A Wright Creed Jenkins & wife Obediah Wooldridge & wife Rob W. Martin & wife Wm Wilkerson & wife Richard Mann & wife & Robert B. Martin & wife	Resident	Fee	73-1/2		near Clover Hill	_ W	10.00		733.00
William M Wright & Chas H Diuguid	Resident	Fee	1/2		Adj Clover Hill		100.00	50.00	50.00
William M Wright	Resident	Fee	12		On P Edward Island	3 SW	10.00	80.00	120.00
Robert C Wright Est	Resident	Fee	73-1/3		Adj John Sears	1 W	8.50	700.00	623.33

Appendix: Appomattox County, Virginia, 1855 Land Tax List:

Isaac Adam District:

Name Of Owner [Continued from prior page]	Amount of tax on the whole tract, at the legal rate	Amount of tax for county purposes	Explanation of alterations during the preceding year, especially from whom transferred	Identification
Helena Wright	1.20			Helen (____) Wright, wife of 1881 William P. Wright of Appomattox County, , a son of Charles Wright, and grandson of Robert Wright, Sr. (Campbell County)
John P Wright	.61			1873 John Patterson Wright of Campbell County, son of 1811 John Wright of Campbell County and grandson of Robert Wright, Sr. (Campbell County)
Pryor Wright Senr Est " "	4.53 .46 1.00		off Branch ? to EB __ & from Lord to Henry F Boison	Estate of 1854 Pryor Rucker Wright, Jr., of Appomattox County, son of 1820 Pryor Wright, Sr., of Prince Edward County and grandson of 1779 John Wright of Prince Edward County
Parker A Wright Creed Jenkins & wife Obediah Wooldridge & wife Rob W. Martin & wife Wm Wilkerson & wife Richard Mann & wife & Robert B. Martin & wife	1.47			Children & children in law of 1815 Robert C. Wright of Prince Edward County, son of 1820 Pryor Wright, Sr., of Prince Edward County and grandson of 1779 John Wright of Prince Edward County
William M Wright & Chas H Diuguid	.10			
William M Wright	.24			1897 William M. Wright of Bedford County, son of 1854 Samuel A. Wright of Appomattox County, grandson of 1820 Pryor Wright, Sr., of Prince Edward County, and great grandson of 1779 John Wright of Prince Edward County
Robert C Wright Est	1.25			Estate of 1815 Robert C. Wright of Prince Edward County, son of 1820 Pryor Wright, Sr., of Prince Edward County and grandson of 1779 John Wright of Prince Edward County

Appendix: Appomattox County, Virginia, 1855 Land Tax List:

Isaac Adam District:

Name Of Owner	Residence	Estate whether held in Fee simple, life &c	No. of Acres	Name of Tract	Description of the land, as to watercourses, mountains and contiguous tracts	Distance and bearing from the courthouse	Value of land per acre, including buildings	Sum added to the land on account if buildings	Total value of the land and buildings
Samuel Wright	Buckingham	Fee	171-1/8		Adj Jno Morris	15 E	5.00	200.00	855.62

Appendix: Appomattox County, Virginia, 1855 Land Tax List:

<u>Isaac Adam District</u>:

Name Of Owner [Continued from prior page]	Amount of tax on the whole tract, at the legal rate	Amount of tax for county purposes	Explanation of alterations during the preceding year, especially from whom transferred	Identification
Samuel Wright	1.71			

Appendix: Appomattox County, Virginia, 1855 Land Tax List:

Town Lots in District of Isaac Adam:

Name Of Owner	Residence	Estate whether in fee simple for life &c	Number of each lot in the town or a description of the part of lot owned	Name of Town	Value of buildings	Value of lots including buildings	Amount of tax on lots at the legal rate	Amount of tax for county purposes
Pryor Wright Sen Est	Resident	Fee	part of lots 24 & 32	Du__ville	500.00	600.00	1.20	

Appendix: Appomattox County, Virginia, 1855 Land Tax List:

Town Lots in District of Isaac Adam:

Name Of Owner [Continued from prior page]	Explanation of alterations during the preceding year especially from whom transferred, and how the owner derived the property	Identification
Pryor Wright Sen Est		Estate of 1854 Pryor Rucker Wright, Jr., of Appomattox County, son of 1820 Pryor Wright, Sr., of Prince Edward County and grandson of 1779 John Wright of Prince Edward County

1856 LAND TAX LIST

APPOMATTOX COUNTY, VIRGINIA

Appendix: Appomattox County, Virginia, 1856 Land Tax List:

Isaac Adam District:

Name Of Owner	Residence	Estate whether held in Fee simple, life &c	No. of Acres	Name of Tract	Description of the land, as to watercourses, mountains and contiguous tracts	Distance and bearing from the courthouse	Value of land per acre, including buildings	Sum added to the land on account of buildings	Total value of the land and buildings
Helena Wright	Resident	Life	100		on Wreck Island	10 NW	6.00	100.00	600.00
John P Wright	Lynchburg	Fee	69-1/2		On Wreck Island	10 NW	4.50		303.75
Pryor Wright Sen Est "	Resident "	Fee "	15-1/2 50		Adj W Patterson Est Adj S D McDearman	25 SE 1/2 W	2.00 10.00		31.00 500.00
William M Wright	Resident	Fee	12		On P Edward Road	3 SW	10.00	80.00	120.00
Robert C Wright Est	Resident	Fee	73-1/3		Adj Jno Sears	1 W	8.50	700.00	623.33
Samuel Wright	Buckingham	Fee	171-1/8		Adj John Morris	15 E	5.00	200.00	855.62
Wm M Wright & Chs H Diuguid	Resident	Fee	1/2		Adj Clover Hill	15 NW	100.00	50.00	50.00
Campbell S Wright	Resident	Life	6		near Clover Hill	1/2 W	15.00		90.00
Fountain C Wright	Resident	Fee	15			1/2 W	15.00		225.00

Appendix: Appomattox County, Virginia, 1856 Land Tax List:

Isaac Adam District:

Name Of Owner [Continued from prior page]	Amount of tax on the whole tract, at the legal rate	Amount of tax for county purposes	Explanation of alterations during the preceding year, especially from whom transferred	Identification
Helena Wright	2.60			Helena (____) Wright, wife of 1881 William P. Wright of Appomattox County, a son of Charles Wright, and grandson of Robert Wright, Sr. (Campbell County)
John P Wright	1.21			1873 John Patterson Wright of Campbell County, son of 1811 John Wright of Campbell County and grandson of Robert Wright, Sr. (Campbell County)
Pryor Wright Senr Est "	.12 2.00			Estate of 1854 Pryor Rucker Wright, Jr., of Appomattox County, son of 1820 Pryor Wright, Sr., of Prince Edward County and grandson of 1779 John Wright of Prince Edward County
William M Wright	.48			1897 William M. Wright of Bedford County, son of 1854 Samuel A. Wright of Appomattox County, grandson of 1820 Pryor Wright, Sr., of Prince Edward County, and great grandson of 1779 John Wright of Prince Edward County
Robert C Wright Est	1.25			Estate of 1815 Robert C. Wright of Prince Edward County, son of 1820 Pryor Wright, Sr., of Prince Edward County and grandson of 1779 John Wright of Prince Edward County
Samuel Wright	1.22			
Wm M Wright & Chs H Duiguid	.20			
Campbell S Wright	.36		From Pryor Wright by will	Campbell S. Wright, son of 1854 Pryor Rucker Wright, Jr., of Appomattox County, grandson of 1820 Pryor Wright, Sr., of Prince Edward County, and great grandson of 1779 John Wright of Prince Edward County
Fountain C Wright	.90		From Pryor Wright by will	Fountain C. Wright, son of 1854 Pryor Rucker Wright, Jr., of Appomattox County, grandson of 1820 Pryor Wright, Sr., of Prince Edward County, and great grandson of 1779 John Wright of Prince Edward County

Appendix: Appomattox County, Virginia, 1856 Land Tax List:

Isaac Adam District:

Name Of Owner	Residence	Estate whether held in Fee simple, life &c	No. of Acres	Name of Tract	Description of the land, as to watercourses, mountains and contiguous tracts	Distance and bearing from the courthouse	Value of land per acre, including buildings	Sum added to the land on account of buildings	Total value of the land and buildings
Gilliam Wright	Resident	Fee	10			1/2 W	15.00		150.00
Mariah Wright	Resident	life	71				15.00	360.00	1065.00

Appendix: Appomattox County, Virginia, 1856 Land Tax List:

Isaac Adam District:

Name Of Owner [Continued from prior page]	Amount of tax on the whole tract, at the legal rate	Amount of tax for county purposes	Explanation of alterations during the preceding year, especially from whom transferred	Identification
Gilliam Wright	.69		From Pryor Wright by will	1864 Gilliam Wright of Appomattox County, son of 1854 Pryor Rucker Wright, Jr., of Appomattox County, grandson of 1820 Pryor Wright, Sr., of Prince Edward County, and great grandson of 1779 John Wright of Prince Edward County
Mariah Wright	4.26		From Pryor Wright by will	Mariah (Turner) Wright, wife of 1854 Pryor Rucker Wright, Jr., of Appomattox County, a son of 1820 Pryor Wright, Sr., of Prince Edward County and grandson of 1779 John Wright of Prince Edward County

Appendix: Appomattox County, Virginia, 1856 Land Tax List:

Town Lots in District of Isaac Adam:

Name Of Owner	Residence	Estate whether in fee simple for life &c	Number of each lot in the town or a description of the part of lot owned	Name of Town	Value of buildings	Value of lots including buildings	Amount of tax on lots at the legal rate	Amount of tax for county purposes
Pryor Wright Est	Resident	Fee	part of lots 24 & 32	Clover Hill	500.00	600.00	2.40	

Appendix: Appomattox County, Virginia, 1856 Land Tax List:

Town Lots in District of Isaac Adam:

Name Of Owner [Continued from prior page]	Explanation of alterations during the preceding year especially from whom transferred, and how the owner derived the property	Identification
Pryor Wright Est		Estate of 1854 Pryor Rucker Wright, Jr., of Appomattox County, son of 1820 Pryor Wright, Sr., of Prince Edward County and grandson of 1779 John Wright of Prince Edward County

1318(012706)

1857 LAND TAX LIST

APPOMATTOX COUNTY, VIRGINIA

Appendix: Appomattox County, Virginia, 1857 Land Tax List:

Anthony A North District:

Name Of Owner	Residence	Estate whether held in Fee simple, life &c	No. of Acres	Name of Tract	Description of the land, as to water-courses, mountains and contiguous tracts	Distance and bearing from the courthouse	Value of land per acre, including buildings	Sum added to the land on account of buildings	Total value of the land and buildings
William W Wright	Resident	Fee			All the interest of David M Wright in a tract of land presently owned by Helena Wright				
Helena Wright	Resident	Life	100		On Wreck Island	10 NW	8.00	100.00	500.00
John P Wright	Lynchburg	Fee	69½		On Wreck Island	10 NW	6.00		417.00
Pryor Wright Sr Est	Resident	Fee	15½		adj Wm P McDermed	5 SE	4.00		608.00
Wm M Wright	Bedford	Fee	12		on Pr Edward Road	3 W	20.00	100.00	240.00
Robert C Wright	Resident	Fee	113		adj Jno Sears	1 W	13.00	200.00	1469.00
Samuel A Wright Est	Resident	Fee	195½		adj George Abbott	2 W	5.00	100.00	977.50
William W Wright & Charles H. Diuguid	Resident	Fee	½		adj Clover Hill			200.00	

1318(012706)

68.

Appendix: Appomattox County, Virginia, 1857 Land Tax List:

Anthony A North District:

Name Of Owner [Continued from prior page]	Amount of tax on the whole tract, at the legal rate	Amount of tax for county purposes	Explanation of alterations during the preceding year, especially from whom transferred	Identification
William W Wright				William Washington Wright, son of 1881 William P. Wright of Appomattox County, grandson of Charles Wright, and great grandson of Robert Wright, Sr. (Campbell County)
Helena Wright	3.20			Helena (____) Wright, wife of 1881 William P. Wright of Appomattox County, a son of Charles Wright, and grandson of Robert Wright, Sr. (Campbell County)
John P Wright	1.67			1873 John Patterson Wright of Campbell County, son of 1811 John Wright of Campbell County and grandson of Robert Wright, Sr. (Campbell County)
Pryor Wright Sr Est	2.43			Estate of 1854 Pryor Rucker Wright, Jr., of Appomattox County, son of 1820 Pryor Wright, Sr., of Prince Edward County and grandson of 1779 John Wright of Prince Edward County
William M Wright	.96			1897 William M. Wright of Bedford County, son of 1854 Samuel A. Wright of Appomattox County, grandson of 1820 Pryor Wright, Sr., of Prince Edward County, and great grandson of 1779 John Wright of Prince Edward County
Robert C Wright	5.88			Estate of 1815 Robert C. Wright of Prince Edward County, son of 1820 Pryor Wright, Sr., of Prince Edward County and grandson of 1779 John Wright of Prince Edward County
Samuel A Wright Est	3.91			Estate of 1854 Samuel A. Wright of Appomattox County, son of 1820 Pryor Wright, Sr., of Prince Edward County and grandson of 1779 John Wright of Prince Edward County
William W Wright Charles H. Diuguid	.80			

Appendix: Appomattox County, Virginia, 1857 Land Tax List:

Anthony A North District:

Name Of Owner	Residence	Estate whether held in Fee simple, life &c	No. of Acres	Name of Tract	Description of the land, as to watercourses, mountains and contiguous tracts	Distance and bearing from the courthouse	Value of land per acre, including buildings	Sum added to the land on account of buildings	Total value of the land and buildings
Campbell F Wright	Resident	Life	6		Near Clover Hill		25.00	50.00	150.00
Fountain C Wright	Resident	Fee	15		Near Clover Hill		15.00		225.00
Gilliam Wright	Resident	Fee	10		Near Clover Hill		15.00		150.00
Mariah Wright	Resident	Fee	71		Near Clover Hill		20.00	500.00	1420.00
"	"	"	15		"		10.00		150.00

Appendix: Appomattox County, Virginia, 1857 Land Tax List:

<u>Anthony A North District</u>:

Name Of Owner [Continued from prior page]	Amount of tax on the whole tract, at the legal rate	Amount of tax for county purposes	Explanation of alterations during the preceding year, especially from whom transferred	Identification
Campbell F Wright	.60			Campbell S. Wright, son of 1854 Pryor Rucker Wright, Jr., of Appomattox County, grandson of 1820 Pryor Wright, Sr., of Prince Edward County, and great grandson of 1779 John Wright of Prince Edward County
Fountain C Wright	.50			Fountain C. Wright, son of 1854 Pryor Rucker Wright, Jr., of Appomattox County, grandson of 1820 Pryor Wright, Sr., of Prince Edward County, and great grandson of 1779 John Wright of Prince Edward County
Gilliam Wright	.60			1864 Gilliam Wright of Appomattox County, son of 1854 Pryor Rucker Wright, Jr., of Appomattox County, grandson of 1820 Pryor Wright, Sr., of Prince Edward County, and great grandson of 1779 John Wright of Prince Edward County
Mariah Wright	5.68			
"	.60		From Lenice ____	Mariah (Turner) Wright, wife of 1854 Pryor Rucker Wright, Jr., of Appomattox County, a son of 1820 Pryor Wright, Sr., of Prince Edward County and grandson of 1779 John Wright of Prince Edward County

Appendix: Appomattox County, Virginia, 1857 Land Tax List:

Town Lots in District of Isaac Adam:

Name Of Owner	Residence	Estate whether in fee simple for life &c	Number of each lot in the town or a description of the part of lot owned	Name of Town	Value of buildings	Value of lots including buildings	Amount of tax on lots at the legal rate	Amount of tax for county purposes
Pryor Wright Est	Resident	Fee	part of lots 24 & 32	Clover Hill	500.00	600.00	2.40	

Appendix: Appomattox County, Virginia, 1857 Land Tax List:

Town Lots in District of Isaac Adam:

Name Of Owner [Continued from prior page]	Explanation of alterations during the preceding year especially from whom transferred, and how the owner derived the property	Identification
Pryor Wright Est		Estate of 1854 Pryor Rucker Wright, Jr., of Appomattox County, son of 1820 Pryor Wright, Sr., of Prince Edward County and grandson of 1779 John Wright of Prince Edward County

1858 LAND TAX LIST

APPOMATTOX COUNTY, VIRGINIA

Appendix: Appomattox County, Virginia, 1858 Land Tax List:

Anthony A North District:

Name Of Owner	Residence	Estate whether held in Fee simple, life &c	No. of Acres	Name of Tract	Description of the land, as to watercourses, mountains and contiguous tracts	Distance and bearing from the courthouse	Value of land per acre, including buildings	Sum added to the land on account of buildings	Total value of the land and buildings
Helena Wright	Resident	Life	100		On Wreck Island	10 NW	8.00	100.00	800.00
John P Wright	Lynchburg	Fee	69½		On Wreck Island	10 NW	6.00		417.00
Pryor Wright Est	Resident	Fee	15½		Adj Wm Patteson	5 SE	4.00		62.00
Wm M Wright	Bedford	Fee	12		on Pr Edward Road	3 W	20.00	100.00	240.00
Robert C Wright	Resident	Fee	113		adj John Sears	1 W	13.00	200.00	1469.00
Samuel A Wright Est	Resident	Fee	195½		adj George Abbott	2 W	5.00	100.00	977.50
William M Wright & Charles H. Diuguid			1/2		Clover Hill				200.00
Campbell S Wright	Resident	Life	6		Near Clover Hill		25.00	50.00	150.00

Appendix: Appomattox County, Virginia, 1858 Land Tax List:

<u>Anthony A North District</u>:

Name Of Owner [Continued from prior page]	Amount of tax on the whole tract, at the legal rate	Amount of tax for county purposes	Explanation of alterations during the preceding year, especially from whom transferred	Identification
Helena Wright	3.20			Helena (____) Wright, wife of 1881 William P. Wright of Appomattox County, a son of Charles Wright, and grandson of Robert Wright, Sr. (Campbell County)
John P Wright	1.67			1873 John Patterson Wright of Campbell County, son of 1811 John Wright of Campbell County and grandson of Robert Wright, Sr. (Campbell County)
Pryor Wright Est	.24			Estate of 1854 Pryor Rucker Wright, Jr., of Appomattox County, son of 1820 Pryor Wright, Sr., of Prince Edward County and grandson of 1779 John Wright of Prince Edward County
Wm M Wright	.96			1897 William M. Wright of Bedford County, son of 1854 Samuel A. Wright of Appomattox County, grandson of 1820 Pryor Wright, Sr., of Prince Edward County, and great grandson of 1779 John Wright of Prince Edward County
Robert C Wright	5.88			Estate of 1815 Robert C. Wright of Prince Edward County, son of 1820 Pryor Wright, Sr., of Prince Edward County and grandson of 1779 John Wright of Prince Edward County
Samuel A Wright Est	3.91			Estate of 1854 Samuel A. Wright of Appomattox County, son of 1820 Pryor Wright, Sr., of Prince Edward County and grandson of 1779 John Wright of Prince Edward County
William M Wright & Charles H. Diuguid	.80			
Campbell S Wright	.60			Campbell S. Wright, son of 1854 Pryor Rucker Wright, Jr., of Appomattox County, grandson of 1820 Pryor Wright, Sr., of Prince Edward County and great grandson of 1779 John Wright of Prince Edward County

Appendix: Appomattox County, Virginia, 1858 Land Tax List:

Anthony A North District:

Name Of Owner	Residence	Estate whether held in Fee simple, life &c	No. of Acres	Name of Tract	Description of the land, as to watercourses, mountains and contiguous tracts	Distance and bearing from the courthouse	Value of land per acre, including buildings	Sum added to the land on account of buildings	Total value of the land and buildings
Fountain C Wright	Resident	Fee	15		Near Clover Hill		15.00		225.00
Gilliam Wright	Resident	Fee	10		Near Clover Hill				150.00
Mariah Wright	Resident	Fee	71		Near Clover Hill		20.00	500.00	1420.00
Mariah Wright	Resident	Fee	15		Near Clover Hill		10.00		150.00
Pryor B Wright	Resident	Fee	148		adj George Abbott	2 W	5.00	100.00	740.00

Appendix: Appomattox County, Virginia, 1858 Land Tax List:

<u>Anthony A North District</u>:

Name Of Owner [Continued from prior page]	Amount of tax on the whole tract, at the legal rate	Amount of tax for county purposes	Explanation of alterations during the preceding year, especially from whom transferred	Identification
Fountain C Wright	.90			Fountain C. Wright, son of 1854 Pryor Rucker Wright, Jr., of Appomattox County, grandson of 1820 Pryor Wright, Sr., of Prince Edward County and great grandson of 1779 John Wright of Prince Edward County
Gilliam Wright	.60			1864 Gilliam Wright of Appomattox County, son of 1854 Pryor Rucker Wright, Jr., of Appomattox County, grandson of 1820 Pryor Wright, Sr., of Prince Edward County and great grandson of 1779 John Wright of Prince Edward County
Mariah Wright	6.66			Mariah (Turner) Wright, wife of 1854 Pryor Rucker Wright, Jr., of Appomattox County, a son of 1820 Pryor Wright, Sr., of Prince Edward County and grandson of 1779 John Wright of Prince Edward County
Mariah Wright	.60			Mariah (Turner) Wright, wife of 1854 Pryor Rucker Wright, Jr., of Appomattox County, a son of 1820 Pryor Wright, Sr., of Prince Edward County and grandson of 1779 John Wright of Prince Edward County
Pryor B Wright	2.96		From Samuel A Wright	1882 Pryor B. Wright of Appomattox County, son of 1854 Samuel A. Wright of Appomattox County, grandson of 1820 Pryor Wright, Sr., of Prince Edward County, and great grandson of 1779 John Wright of Prince Edward County

Appendix: Appomattox County, Virginia, 1858 Land Tax List:

Town Lots District of Anthony A North:

Name Of Owner	Residence	Estate whether in fee simple for life &c	Number of each lot in the town or a description of the part of lot owned	Name of Town	Value of buildings	Value of lots including buildings	Amount of tax on lots at the legal rate	Amount of tax for county purposes
Pryor Wright Est	Resident		Lots 24 & 32	Clover Hill	500.00	600.00	2.40	

Appendix: Appomattox County, Virginia, 1858 Land Tax List:

Town Lots District of Anthony A North:

Name Of Owner [Continued from prior page]	Explanation of alterations during the preceding year especially from whom transferred, and how the owner derived the property	Identification
Pryor Wright Est		Estate of 1854 Pryor Rucker Wright, Jr., of Appomattox County, son of 1820 Pryor Wright, Sr., of Prince Edward County and grandson of 1779 John Wright of Prince Edward County

1859 LAND TAX LIST

APPOMATTOX COUNTY, VIRGINIA

Appendix: Appomattox County, Virginia, 1859 Land Tax List:

Anthony A North District:

Name Of Owner	Residence	Estate whether held in Fee simple, life &c	No. of Acres	Name of Tract	Description of the land, as to watercourses, mountains and contiguous tracts	Distance and bearing from the courthouse	Value of land per acre, including buildings	Sum added to the land on account of buildings	Total value of the land and buildings
Wm W Wright	Resident	Fee			all the interest of David M Wright in the land of William Wright deceased				
Helena Wright	Resident	Life	100		On Wreck Island	10 NW	8.00	100.00	800.00
John P Wright	Lynchburg	Fee	69-1/2		On Wreck Island	10 NW	6.00		417.00
Pryor Wright Est	Resident	Fee	15-1/2		Adj Wm Patteson	5 SE	4.00		62.00
Wm M Wright	Bedford	Fee	12		on Pr Edward Road	3 W	20.00	100.00	240.00
Robert C Wright Est	Resident	Fee	113		adj John Sears	1 W	13.00	200.00	1469.00
William M Wright & Charles H. Diuguid	Resident	Fee	1/2		Clover Hill				200.00
Campbell S Wright	Resident	Life	6		Near Clover Hill		25.00	50.00	150.00

Appendix: Appomattox County, Virginia, 1859 Land Tax List:

Anthony A North District:

Name Of Owner [Continued from prior page]	Amount of tax on the whole tract, at the legal rate	Amount of tax for county purposes	Explanation of alterations during the preceding year, especially from whom transferred	Identification
Wm W Wright				William Washington Wright, son of 1881 William P. Wright of Appomattox County, grandson of Charles Wright, and great grandson of Robert Wright, Sr. (Campbell County)
Helena Wright	3.20			Helena (____) Wright, wife of 1881 William P. Wright of Appomattox County, a son of Charles Wright, and grandson of Robert Wright, Sr. (Campbell County)
John P Wright	1.67			1873 John Patterson Wright of Campbell County, son of 1811 John Wright of Campbell County and grandson of Robert Wright, Sr. (Campbell County)
Pryor Wright Est	.24			Estate of 1854 Pryor Rucker Wright, Jr., of Appomattox County, son of 1820 Pryor Wright, Sr., of Prince Edward County and grandson of 1779 John Wright of Prince Edward County
Wm M Wright	.96			1897 William M. Wright of Bedford County, son of 1854 Samuel A. Wright of Appomattox County, grandson of 1820 Pryor Wright, Sr., of Prince Edward County, and great grandson of 1779 John Wright of Prince Edward County
Robert C Wright Est	5.88			Estate of 1815 Robert C. Wright of Prince Edward County, son of 1820 Pryor Wright, Sr., of Prince Edward County and grandson of 1779 John Wright of Prince Edward County
William M Wright & Charles H. Diuguid	.80			
Campbell S Wright	.67			Campbell S. Wright, son of 1854 Pryor Rucker Wright, Jr., of Appomattox County, grandson of 1820 Pryor Wright, Sr., of Prince Edward County, and great grandson of 1779 John Wright of Prince Edward County

Appendix: Appomattox County, Virginia, 1859 Land Tax List:

Anthony A North District:

Name Of Owner	Residence	Estate whether held in Fee simple, life &c	No. of Acres	Name of Tract	Description of the land, as to watercourses, mountains and contiguous tracts	Distance and bearing from the courthouse	Value of land per acre, including buildings	Sum added to the land on account of buildings	Total value of the land and buildings
Fountain C Wright	Resident	Fee	15		Near Clover Hill		15.00		225.00
Gilliam Wright	Resident	Fee	10		Near Clover Hill		15.00		150.00
Mariah Wright	Resident	Fee	71		Near Clover Hill		20.00	500.00	1420.00
Pryor B Wright	Resident	Fee	148		adj George Abbott	2 W	5.00	100.00	740.00

Appendix: Appomattox County, Virginia, 1859 Land Tax List:

Anthony A North District:

Name Of Owner [Continued from prior page]	Amount of tax on the whole tract, at the legal rate	Amount of tax for county purposes	Explanation of alter- ations during the pre- ceding year, especially from whom transferred	Identification
Fountain C Wright	.90			Fountain C. Wright, son of 1854 Pryor Rucker Wright, Jr., of Appomattox County, grandson of 1820 Pryor Wright, Sr., of Prince Edward County, and great grandson of 1779 John Wright of Prince Edward County
Gilliam Wright	.60			1864 Gilliam Wright of Appomattox County, son of 1854 Pryor Rucker Wright, Jr., of Appomattox County, grandson of 1820 Pryor Wright, Sr., of Prince Edward County, and great grandson of 1779 John Wright of Prince Edward County
Mariah Wright	5.68			Mariah (Turner) Wright, wife of 1854 Pryor Rucker Wright, Jr., of Appomattox County, a son of 1820 Pryor Wright, Sr., of Prince Edward County and grandson of 1779 John Wright of Prince Edward County
Pryor B Wright	2.96			1882 Pryor B. Wright of Appomattox County, son of 1854 Samuel A. Wright of Appomattox County, grandson of 1820 Pryor Wright, Sr., of Prince Edward County, and great grandson of 1779 John Wright of Prince Edward County

Appendix: Appomattox County, Virginia, 1859 Land Tax List:

Town Lots District of Anthony A North:

Name Of Owner	Residence	Estate whether in fee simple for life &c	Number of each lot in the town or a description of the part of lot owned	Name of Town	Value of buildings	Value of lots including buildings	Amount of tax on lots at the legal rate	Amount of tax for county purposes
Pryor Wright Est	Resident	Fee	Lot 24 & 32	Clover Hill	500.00	600.00	2.40	

Appendix: Appomattox County, Virginia, 1859 Land Tax List:

Town Lots District of Anthony A North:

Name Of Owner [Continued from prior page]	Explanation of alterations during the preceding year especially from whom transferred, and how the owner derived the property	Identification
Pryor Wright Est		Estate of 1854 Pryor Rucker Wright, Jr., of Appomattox County, son of 1820 Pryor Wright, Sr., of Prince Edward County and grandson of 1779 John Wright of Prince Edward County

1318(012706)

1860 LAND TAX LIST

APPOMATTOX COUNTY, VIRGINIA

Appendix: Appomattox County, Virginia, 1860 Land Tax List:

<u>Anthony A North District</u>:

Name Of Owner	Residence	Estate whether held in Fee simple, life &c	No. of Acres	Name of Tract	Description of the land, as to watercourses, mountains and contiguous tracts	Distance and bearing from the courthouse	Value of land per acre, including buildings	Sum added to the land on account of buildings	Total value of the land and buildings
Benjamin E. Wright & Wm W Wright	Resident "	Fee "			all the interest of David M Wright in a tract of land owned by Helenner Wright all the interest of Richard T Wright in the same tract				
Heleann Wright	Resident	Life	100		On Wreck Island	10 NW	8.00	100.00	800.00
Robert C Wright Est	Resident	Fee	150		On Appamattox	6 E	4.00	50.00	600.00
John P Wright	Lynchburg	Fee	69-1/2		On Wreck Island	10 NW	6.00		417.00
Pryor Wright Est	Resident	Fee	15-1/2		adj Wm Patteson	5 SE	4.00		62.00
Wm M Wright	Bedford	Fee	12		on Pr Edward Road	3 W	20.00	100.00	240.00
Robert C Wright Est	Resident	Fee	113		adj John Sears	1 W	13.00	200.00	1467.00

Appendix: Appomattox County, Virginia, 1860 Land Tax List:

Anthony A North District:

Name Of Owner [Continued from prior page]	Amount of tax on the whole tract, at the legal rate	Amount of tax for county purposes	Explanation of alterations during the preceding year, especially from whom transferred	Identification
Benjamin E. Wright & Wm W Wright				1880 Benjamin Edward Wright of Amherst County, son of 1881 William P. Wright of Appomattox County, grandson of Charles Wright, and great grandson of Robert Wright, Sr. (Campbell County) and William Washington Wright, son of 1881 William P. Wright of Appomattox County, grandson of Charles Wright, and great grandson of Robert Wright, Sr. (Campbell County)
Heleann Wright	3.20			Helena (____) Wright, wife of 1881 William P. Wright of Appomattox County, a son of Charles Wright, and grandson of Robert Wright, Sr. (Campbell County)
Robert C Wright Est	2.40			Estate of 1815 Robert C. Wright of Prince Edward County, son of 1820 Pryor Wright, Sr., of Prince Edward County and grandson of 1779 John Wright of Prince Edward County
John P Wright	1.67			1873 John Patterson Wright of Campbell County, son of 1811 John Wright of Campbell County and grandson of Robert Wright, Sr. (Campbell County)
Pryor Wright Est	.24			Estate of 1854 Pryor Rucker Wright, Jr., of Appomattox County, son of 1820 Pryor Wright, Sr., of Prince Edward County and grandson of 1779 John Wright of Prince Edward County
Wm M Wright	.96			1897 William M. Wright of Bedford County, son of 1854 Samuel A. Wright of Appomattox County, grandson of 1820 Pryor Wright, Sr., of Prince Edward County, and great grandson of 1779 John Wright of Prince Edward County
Robert C Wright Est	5.88			Estate of 1815 Robert C. Wright of Prince Edward County, son of 1820 Pryor Wright, Sr., of Prince Edward County and grandson of 1779 John Wright of Prince Edward County

Appendix: Appomattox County, Virginia, 1860 Land Tax List:

Anthony A North District:

Name Of Owner	Residence	Estate whether held in Fee simple, life &c	No. of Acres	Name of Tract	Description of the land, as to watercourses, mountains and contiguous tracts	Distance and bearing from the courthouse	Value of land per acre, including buildings	Sum added to the land on account of buildings	Total value of the land and buildings
William M Wright & Charles H. Diuguid	Resident	Fee	1/2		Clover Hill				200.00
Campbell S Wright	Resident	Life	6		Near Clover Hill		25.00	50.00	150.00
Fountain C Wright	Resident	Fee	15		Near Clover Hill		15.00		225.00
Gilliam Wright	Resident	Fee	10		Near Clover Hill		15.00		150.00
Mariah Wright	Resident	Fee	71		Near Clover Hill		20.00	500.00	1420.00
Pryor B Wright	Resident	Fee	148		adj George Abbott	2 SW	5.00	100.00	740.00

1318(012706)

94.

Appendix: Appomattox County, Virginia, 1860 Land Tax List:

Anthony A North District:

Name Of Owner [Continued from prior page]	Amount of tax on the whole tract, at the legal rate	Amount of tax for county purposes	Explanation of alterations during the preceding year, especially from whom transferred	Identification
William M Wright & Charles H. Diuguid	.80			
Campbell S Wright	.60			Campbell S. Wright, son of 1854 Pryor Rucker Wright, Jr., of Appomattox County, grandson of 1820 Pryor Wright, Sr., of Prince Edward County and great grandson of 1779 John Wright of Prince Edward County
Fountain C Wright	.90			Fountain C. Wright, son of 1854 Pryor Rucker Wright, Jr., of Appomattox County, grandson of 1820 Pryor Wright, Sr., of Prince Edward County and great grandson of 1779 John Wright of Prince Edward County
Gilliam Wright	.60			1864 Gilliam Wright of Appomattox County, son of 1854 Pryor Rucker Wright, Jr., of Appomattox County, grandson of 1820 Pryor Wright, Sr., of Prince Edward County, and great grandson of 1779 John Wright of Prince Edward County
Mariah Wright	5.68			Mariah (Turner) Wright, wife of 1854 Pryor Rucker Wright, Jr., of Appomattox, a son of 1820 Pryor Wright, Sr., of Prince Edward County and grandson of 1779 John Wright of Prince Edward County
Pryor B Wright	2.96			1882 Pryor B. Wright of Appomattox County, son of 1854 Samuel A. Wright of Appomattox County, grandson of 1820 Pryor Wright, Sr., of Prince Edward County, and great grandson of 1779 John Wright of Prince Edward County

Appendix: Appomattox County, Virginia, 1860 Land Tax List:

Town Lots District of Anthony A North:

Name Of Owner	Residence	Estate whether in fee simple for life &c	Number of each lot in the town or a description of the part of lot owned	Name of Town	Value of buildings	Value of lots including buildings	Amount of tax on lots at the legal rate	Amount of tax for county purposes
Pryor Wright Est	Resident	Fee	Lot 24 & 32	Clover Hill	500.00	600.00	2.40	

Appendix: Appomattox County, Virginia, 1860 Land Tax List:

Town Lots District of Anthony A North:

Name Of Owner [Continued from prior page]	Explanation of alterations during the preceding year especially from whom transferred, and how the owner derived the property	Identification
Pryor Wright Est		Estate of 1854 Pryor Rucker Wright, Jr., of Appomattox County, son of 1820 Pryor Wright, Sr., of Prince Edward County and grandson of 1779 John Wright of Prince Edward County

1861 LAND TAX LIST

APPOMATTOX COUNTY, VIRGINIA

Appendix: Appomattox County, Virginia, 1861 Land Tax List:

Samuel J Walker District:

Name of the Person by himself or by his tenant has the free-hold in possession of the land charged	Residence of the owner of the tract of land	Nature of the owner's estate whether held in fee or for life	Number of acres in said tract	Name of the tract and description of the land, as to water courses, mountains or other places on or near which it lies	Distance and bearing from the court house Bearing from C. H.	Miles	Total value of land per acre including buildings	The sum included in the value of each tract of land on account of buildings	Total value of the land and buildings
Benj & William W Wright	Resident	fee		all the interest of David M Wright in a tract of land owned by Helena Wright					
Same	"	"		all the interest of Richd T Wright in same tract					
William Wrights Est	Resident	life	100	On Wreck Island Ck	NW	10	8.00	100.00	800.00
John P Wright	Campbell	fee	69-1/2	On Wreck Island Crk	NW	10	6.00		417.00
Pryor Wright Est	Resident	fee	15-1/2	adj Wm Patteson	SE	5	4.00		62.00
William M Wright	Bedford	fee	12	near Appomattox Depot	W	3	20.00	100.00	240.00
Ro C Wrights Est	Resident	fee							
William M Wright & Ch H Diuguid	Resident	fee	1/2	Clover Hill					200.00

Appendix: Appomattox County, Virginia, 1861 Land Tax List:

Samuel J Walker District:

Name of the Person [Continued from prior page]	The amount of tax on the whole tract, at forty cents on every $100 value thereof	Explanation of alterations during the preceding year, especially from whom transferred, and when and how the owner derived the land, and why, and upon what authority any alteration was made	Identification
Benj & William W Wright Same			1880 Benjamin Edward Wright of Amherst County, son of 1881 William P. Wright of Appomattox County, grandson of Charles Wright, and great grandson of Robert Wright, Sr. (Campbell County) and William Washington Wright, son of 1881 William P. Wright of Appomattox County, grandson of Charles Wright, and great grandson of Robert Wright, Sr. (Campbell County)
William Wrights Est	3.20		1881 William P. Wright of Appomattox County, son of Charles Wright and grandson of Robert Wright, Sr. (Campbell County)
John P Wright	1.67		1873 John Patterson Wright of Campbell County, son of 1811 John Wright of Campbell County and grandson of Robert Wright, Sr. (Campbell County)
Pryor Wright Est	.25		Estate of 1854 Pryor Rucker Wright, Jr., of Appomattox County, son of 1820 Pryor Wright, Sr., of Prince Edward County and grandson of 1779 John Wright of Prince Edward County
William M Wright	.96		1897 William M. Wright of Bedford County, son of 1854 Samuel A. Wright of Appomattox County, grandson of 1820 Pryor Wright, Sr., of Prince Edward County, and great grandson of 1779 John Wright of Prince Edward County
Ro C Wrights Est		off to Willis Impt(?) quantity Correction	Estate of 1815 Robert C. Wright of Prince Edward County, son of 1820 Pryor Wright, Sr., of Prince Edward County, and grandson of 1779 John Wright of Prince Edward County
William M Wright & Charles H. Diuguid	.80		

Appendix: Appomattox County, Virginia, 1861 Land Tax List:

<u>Samuel J Walker District</u>:

Name of the Person by himself or by his tenant has the free-hold in possession of the land charged	Residence of the owner of the tract of land	Nature of the owner's estate whether held in fee or for life	Number of acres in said tract	Name of the tract and description of the land, as to water courses, mountains or other places on or near which it lies	Distance and bearing from the court house Bearing from C. H.	Miles	Total value of land per acre including buildings	The sum included in the value of each tract of land on account of buildings	Total value of the land and buildings
Campbell S Wright	Resident	life	6	Near Clover Hill			25.00	50.00	150.00
Fountain C Wright	Resident	fee	15	Near Clover Hill			15.00		225.00
Gilliam Wright	Resident	fee	10	Near Clover Hill			15.00		150.00
Mariah Wright	Resident	fee	71	Near Clover Hill			20.00	500.00	1420.00
Pryor B Wright	Resident	fee	148	adj Geo Abbott	SW	2	5.00	100.00	740.00

Appendix: Appomattox County, Virginia, 1861 Land Tax List:

Samuel J Walker District:

Name of the Person [Continued from prior page]	The amount of tax on the whole tract, at forty cents on every $100 value thereof	Explanation of alterations during the preceding year, especially from whom transferred, and when and how the owner derived the land, and why, and upon what authority any alteration was made	Identification
Campbell S Wright	.60		Campbell S. Wright, son of 1854 Pryor Rucker Wright, Jr., of Appomattox, grandson of 1820 Pryor Wright, Sr., of Prince Edward County County, and great grandson of 1779 John Wright of Prince Edward County
Fountain C Wright	.90		Fountain C. Wright, son of 1854 Pryor Rucker Wright, Jr., of Appomattox, grandson of 1820 Pryor Wright, Sr., of Prince Edward County County, and great grandson of 1779 John Wright of Prince Edward County
Gilliam Wright	.60		1864 Gilliam Wright of Appomattox County, son of 1854 Pryor Rucker Wright, Jr., of Appomattox, grandson of 1820 Pryor Wright, Sr., of Prince Edward County County, and great grandson of 1779 John Wright of Prince Edward County
Mariah Wright	5.68		Mariah (Turner) Wright, wife of 1854 Pryor Rucker Wright, Jr., of Appomattox County, a son of 1820 Pryor Wright, Sr., of Prince Edward County and grandson of 1779 John Wright of Prince Edward County
Pryor B Wright	2.96		1882 Pryor B. Wright of Appomattox County, son of 1854 Samuel A. Wright of Appomattox County, grandson of 1820 Pryor Wright, Sr., of Prince Edward County, and great grandson of 1779 John Wright of Prince Edward County

Appendix: Appomattox County, Virginia, 1861 Land Tax List:

Town Lots District of Samuel W Walker:

Name of the Person Who by himself or by his tenant has the freehold of the land charged to possession	Residence of the owner of the tract of land	Nature of the owner's estate whether in fee simple for life	Number of each lot in the town, or a description of the part of lot owned	Name of the town in which the lot is situated	Value of buildings on the lot	Value of lots including buildings	The amount of tax on lots at 100 cents on every $100 value thereof
Pryor Wrights est	Resident	Fee	Lot No 24 & 32	Clover Hill	500.00	600.00	2.40

Appendix: Appomattox County, Virginia, 1861 Land Tax List:

<u>Town Lots District of Samuel W Walker</u>:

Name of the Person [Continued from prior page]	Explanation of alterations during the preceding year especially from whom transferred, and when and how the owner acquired the lot, and why, and upon what authority any alteration was made	Identification
Pryor Wrights est		Estate of 1854 Pryor Rucker Wright, Jr., of Appomattox County, son of 1820 Pryor Wright, Sr., of Prince Edward County and grandson of 1779 John Wright of Prince Edward County

1318(012706)

1862 LAND TAX LIST

APPOMATTOX COUNTY, VIRGINIA

Appendix: Appomattox County, Virginia, 1862 Land Tax List:

<u>Samuel J Walker District</u>:

Name of the Person by himself or by his tenant has the free-hold in possession of the land charged	Residence of the owner of the tract of land	Nature of the owner's estate whether held in fee or for life	Number of acres in said tract	Name of the tract and description of the land, as to water courses, mountains or other places on or near which it lies	Distance and bearing from the court house Bearing from C. H.	Miles	Total value of land per acre including buildings	The sum included in the value of each tract of land on account of buildings	Total value of the land and buildings
Benjamin E & William W Wright	Resident	fee		all the interest of David M Wright in a tract of land formerly owned by Helena Wright					
ditto	"	"		all the interest of Richard T Wright on the same estate					
Helena Wrights Estate	Resident	Life	100	On Wreck Island Cr	NW	10	8.00	100.00	800.00
John P Wright	Campbell	fee	69-1/2	On Wreck Island Cr	NW	10	6.00		417.00
Pryor Wrights Estate	Resident	fee	15-1/2	adj Wm Patterson	SE	5	4.00		62.00
Wm M Wright	Bedford	fee	12	near Appomattox Depot	SW	3	20.00	100.00	240.00
Wm M Wright & Charles H Duigiud (Colored)	Resident	fee	1/2	Clover Hill					200.00
Campbell S Wright	Resident	Life	6	Near Clover Hill			25.00	50.00	150.00

1318(012706)

108.

Appendix: Appomattox County, Virginia, 1862 Land Tax List:

<u>Samuel J Walker District</u>:

Name of the Person [Continued from prior page]	The amount of tax on the whole tract, at forty cents on every $100 value thereof	Explanation of alterations during the preceding year, especially from whom transferred, and when and how the owner derived the land, and why, and upon what authority any alteration was made	Identification
Benjamin E & William W Wright ditto			1880 Benjamin Edward Wright of Amherst County, son of 1881 William P. Wright of Appomattox County, grandson of Charles Wright, and great grandson of Robert Wright, Sr. (Campbell County) and William Washington Wright, son of 1881 William P. Wright of Appomattox County, grandson of Charles Wright, and great grandson of Robert Wright, Sr. (Campbell County)
Helena Wrights Estate	4.80		Helena (____) Wright, wife of 1881 William P. Wright of Appomattox County, a son of Charles Wright, and grandson of Robert Wright, Sr. (Campbell County)
John P Wright	2.50		1873 John Patterson Wright of Campbell County, son of 1811 John Wright of Campbell County and grandson of Robert Wright, Sr. (Campbell County)
Pryor Wrights Estate	.37		Estate of 1854 Pryor Rucker Wright, Jr., of Appomattox County, son of 1820 Pryor Wright, Sr., of Prince Edward County and grandson of 1779 John Wright of Prince Edward County
Wm M Wright	1.44		1897 William M. Wright of Bedford County, son of 1854 Samuel A. Wright of Appomattox County, grandson of 1820 Pryor Wright, Sr., of Prince Edward County, and great grandson of 1779 John Wright of Prince Edward County
Wm M Wright & Charles H Duigiud (Colored)	1.20		
Campbell S Wright	.90		Campbell S. Wright, son of 1854 Pryor Rucker Wright, Jr., of Appomattox County, grandson of 1820 Pryor Wright, Sr., of Prince Edward County, and great grandson of 1779 John Wright of Prince Edward County

Appendix: Appomattox County, Virginia, 1862 Land Tax List:

Samuel J Walker District:

Name of the Person by himself or by his tenant has the free-hold in possession of the land charged	Residence of the owner of the tract of land	Nature of the owner's estate whether held in fee or for life	Number of acres in said tract	Name of the tract and description of the land, as to water courses, mountains or other places on or near which it lies	Distance and bearing from the court house Bearing from C. H.	Miles	Total value of land per acre including buildings	The sum included in the value of each tract of land on account of buildings	Total value of the land and buildings
Fountain C Wright	Resident	fee	15	Near Clover Hill			15.00		225.00
Gilliam Wright	Resident	fee	10	Near Clover Hill			15.00		150.00
Maria Wright	Resident	fee	71	Near Clover Hill			20.00	500.00	1420.00
Pryor B Wright	Resident	fee	148	adj Geo Abbott	SW	2	7.00	296.00	1036.00

Appendix: Appomattox County, Virginia, 1862 Land Tax List:

Samuel J Walker District:

Name of the Person [Continued from prior page]	The amount of tax on the whole tract, at forty cents on every $100 value thereof	Explanation of alterations during the preceding year, especially from whom transferred, and when and how the owner derived the land, and why, and upon what authority any alteration was made	Identification
Fountain C Wright	1.35		Fountain C. Wright, son of 1854 Pryor Rucker Wright, Jr., of Appomattox County, grandson of 1820 Pryor Wright, Sr., of Prince Edward County, and great grandson of 1779 John Wright of Prince Edward County
Gilliam Wright	.90		1864 Gilliam Wright of Appomattox County, son of 1854 Pryor Rucker Wright, Jr., of Appomattox County, grandson of 1820 Pryor Wright, Sr., of Prince Edward County, and great grandson of 1779 John Wright of Prince Edward County
Mariah Wright	8.52		Mariah (Turner) Wright, wife of 1854 Pryor Rucker Wright, Jr., of Appomattox County, a son of 1820 Pryor Wright, Sr., of Prince Edward County and grandson of 1779 John Wright of Prince Edward County
Pryor B Wright	6.22	196 dollars added for new buildings	1882 Pryor B. Wright of Appomattox County, son of 1854 Samuel A. Wright of Appomattox County, grandson of 1820 Pryor Wright, Sr., of Prince Edward County, and great grandson of 1779 John Wright of Prince Edward County

Appendix: Appomattox County, Virginia, 1862 Land Tax List:

Town Lots District of Samuel W Walker:

Name of the Person	Residence							The amount of
Who by himself or by his tenant has the freehold of the land charged to possession	of the owner of the tract of land	Nature of the owner's estate whether in fee simple for life	Number of each lot in the town, or a description of the part of lot owned	Name of the town in which the lot is situated	Value of buildings on the lot	Value of lots including buildings		tax on lots at 100 cents on every $100 value thereof
Pryor Wrights Estate	Resident	Fee	Part of 32 & part of 24	Clover Hill	500.00	600.00	3.60	

Appendix: Franklin County, Virginia, 1862 Land Tax List:

Town Lots District of Samuel W Walker:

Name of the Person [Continued from prior page]	Explanation of alterations during the preceding year especially from whom transferred, and when and how the owner acquired the lot, and why, and upon what authority any alteration was made	Identification
Pryor Wrights Estate		Estate of 1854 Pryor Rucker Wright, Jr., of Appomattox County, son of 1820 Pryor Wright, Sr., of Prince Edward County and grandson of 1779 John Wright of Prince Edward County

1863 LAND TAX LIST

APPOMATTOX COUNTY, VIRGINIA

Appendix: Appomattox County, Virginia, 1863 Land Tax List:

Samuel J Walker District:

Name of the Person Who by himself or by his tenant has the freehold in possession of the land charged	Residence of the owner of the tract of land	Nature of the owner's estate whether held in fee or for life	Number of acres in said tract	Name of the tract and description of the land, as to water courses, mountains or other places on or near which it lies	Distance and bearing from the court house Bearing from C. H.	Miles	Total value of land per acre including buildings	The sum included in the value of each tract of land on account of buildings	Total value of the land and buildings
Benj E & Wm W Wright	Resident	Fee		All the interest of David M Wright in a tract of land formerly owned by Helena Wright					
ditto	"	"		All the int. of Richd T Wright on the same land					
Helena Wrights Est	Resident	Life	100	On Wreck Island Cr	NW	10	8.00	100.00	800.00
Jno P Wright	Campbell	Fee	69-1/2	On Waters of W I Creek	NW	10	6.00		417.00
Pryor Wright Est	Resident	Fee	15-1/2	adj Wm Patteson	SE	5	4.00		62.00
Wm M Wright	Bedford	Fee	12	Near Appomattox Depot	SW	3	20.00	100.00	240.00
Wm M Wright & Charles H Duiguid color	Residt	Fee	1/2	Adj Clover Hill					200.00

Appendix: Appomattox County, Virginia, 1863 Land Tax List:

Samuel J Walker District:

Name of the Person [Continued from prior page]	The amount of tax on the whole tract, at forty cents on every $100 value thereof	Explanation of alterations during the preceding year, especially from whom transferred, and when and how the owner derived the land, and why, and upon what authority any alteration was made	Identification
Benj E & Wm W Wright ditto			1880 Benjamin Edward Wright of Amherst County, son of 1881 William P. Wright of Appomattox County, grandson of Charles Wright, and great grandson of Robert Wright, Sr. (Campbell County) and William Washington Wright, son of 1881 William P. Wright of Appomattox County, grandson of Charles Wright, and great grandson of Robert Wright, Sr. (Campbell County)
Helena Wrights Est	8.00		Estate of Helena (____) Wright, wife of 1881 William P. Wright of Appomattox County, a son of Charles Wright, and grandson of Robert Wright, Sr. (Campbell County)
Jno P Wright	4.17		1873 John Patterson Wright of Campbell County, son of 1811 John Wright of Campbell County and grandson of Robert Wright, Sr. (Campbell County)
Pryor Wright Est	.62		Estate of 1854 Pryor Rucker Wright, Jr., of Appomattox County, son of 1820 Pryor Wright, Sr., of Prince Edward County and grandson of 1779 John Wright of Prince Edward County
Wm M Wright	2.40		1897 William M. Wright of Bedford County, son of 1854 Samuel A. Wright of Appomattox County, grandson of 1820 Pryor Wright, Sr., of Prince Edward County, and great grandson of 1779 John Wright of Prince Edward County
Wm M Wright & Charles H Diuguid color	2.00		

Appendix: Appomattox County, Virginia, 1863 Land Tax List:

Samuel J Walker District:

Name of the Person Who by himself or by his tenant has the freehold in possession of the land charged	Residence of the owner of the tract of land	Nature of the owner's estate whether held in fee or for life	Number of acres in said tract	Name of the tract and description of the land, as to water courses, mountains or other places on or near which it lies	Distance and bearing from the court house Bearing from C. H.	Miles	Total value of land per acre including buildings	The sum included in the value of each tract of land on account of buildings	Total value of the land and buildings
Campbell S Wright	Resident	Life	6	At Clover Hill			25.00	50.00	150.00
Fountain C Wright	Resident	Fee	15	At Clover Hill			15.00		225.00
Gilliam Wright	Resident	Fee	10	At Clover Hill			15.00		150.00
Maria Wright	Resident	Fee	71	At Clover Hill			20.00	500.00	1420.00
Pryor B Wright	Resident	Fee	148	adj Geo Abbott	SW	2	7.00	296.00	1036.00

Appendix: Appomattox County, Virginia, 1863 Land Tax List:

<u>Samuel J Walker District</u>:

Name of the Person [Continued from prior page]	The amount of tax on the whole tract, at forty cents on every $100 value thereof	Explanation of alterations during the preceding year, especially from whom transferred, and when and how the owner derived the land, and why, and upon what authority any alteration was made	Identification
Campbell S Wright	1.50		Campbell S. Wright, son of 1854 Pryor Rucker Wright, Jr., of Appomattox County, grandson of 1820 Pryor Wright, Sr., of Prince Edward County, and great grandson of 1779 John Wright of Prince Edward County
Fountain C Wright	2.25		Fountain C. Wright, son of 1854 Pryor Rucker Wright, Jr., of Appomattox County, grandson of 1820 Pryor Wright, Sr., of Prince Edward County, and great grandson of 1779 John Wright of Prince Edward County
Gilliam Wright	1.50		1864 Gilliam Wright of Appomattox County, son of 1854 Pryor Rucker Wright, Jr., of Appomattox County, grandson of 1820 Pryor Wright, Sr., of Prince Edward County, and great grandson of 1779 John Wright of Prince Edward County
Maria Wright	14.20		Mariah (Turner) Wright, wife of 1854 Pryor Rucker Wright, Jr., of Appomattox County, a son of 1820 Pryor Wright, Sr., of Prince Edward County and grandson of 1779 John Wright of Prince Edward County
Pryor B Wright	10.36		1882 Pryor B. Wright of Appomattox County, son of 1854 Samuel A. Wright of Appomattox County, grandson of 1820 Pryor Wright, Sr., of Prince Edward County, and great grandson of 1779 John Wright of Prince Edward County

Appendix: Appomattox County, Virginia, 1863 Land Tax List:

Town Lots District of Samuel W Walker:

Name of the Person Who by himself or by his tenant has the freehold of the land charged to possession	Residence of the owner of the tract of land	Nature of the owner's estate whether in fee simple for life	Number of each lot in the town, or a description of the part of lot owned	Name of the town in which the lot is situated	Value of buildings on the lot	Value of lots including buildings	The amount of tax on lots at 100 cents on every $100 value thereof
Pryor Wrights Est	Resident	Fee	Part of Lots Lots 24 & 32	Clover Hill	500.00	600.00	6.00

Appendix: Appomattox County, Virginia, 1863 Land Tax List:

Town Lots District of Samuel W Walker:

Name of the Person [Continued from prior page]	Explanation of alterations during the preceding year especially from whom transferred, and when and how the owner acquired the lot, and why, and upon what authority any alteration was made	Identification
Pryor Wrights Est		Estate of 1854 Pryor Rucker Wright, Jr., of Appomattox County, son of 1820 Pryor Wright, Sr., of Prince Edward County and grandson of 1779 John Wright of Prince Edward County

INDEX

WRIGHT FAMILY

DEATH RECORDS

APPOMATTOX COUNTY, VIRGINIA

1852 to 1920

Revised as of March 25, 2006

Introduction To Appendix: Death Records for Appomattox County, Virginia

This document is an appendix to a larger work titled Sorting Some Of The Wrights Of Southern Virginia. The work is divided into parts for each family of Wrights that has been researched. Each part is divided into two sections; the first section is text discussing the family and the evidence supporting the relationships and the second section is a descendants chart summarizing the relationships and information known about each individual.

The appendices to the work (of which this document is one) present source records for persons named Wright by county and by type of record with the identification of the person named and their Wright ancestors to the extent known.

The source for the records listed in this appendix is the following:

1) Appomattox County, Virginia, Death Records, available from the Commonwealth of Virginia, Department of Health, Division of Vital Records, P.O. Box 1000, Richmond, Virginia 23208-1000.

The identification of a person or their ancestor by year and county indicates their year of death and county of residence at death. For example, "1763 Thomas Wright of Bedford County" indicates that this was the Thomas Wright who died in 1763 in Bedford County. If no state is listed after the county, the state is Virginia; counties in states other than Virginia will have a state listed after the county, as in "1876 William S. Wright of Highland County, Ohio".

A parenthetical after the name indicates an identification of the person when a place of death is not yet known, as in "John Wright (Goochland County Carpenter)". A county in parentheses after the name indicates the county with which that person was most identified when no evidence of the place of death has yet been found, as in "Grief Wright (Bedford County)".

All or portions of the text and descendants charts for each Wright family identified are available from the author:

Robert N. Grant
15 Campo Bello Court   (H) 650-854-0895
Menlo Park, California 94025   (O) 650-614-3800

This is a work in progress and I would be most interested in receiving additional information about any of the persons identified in these records in order to correct any errors or expand on the information given.

0855(032506)

Appendix: Appomattox County, Virginia, Death Records

Book/Page	Date	Decedent	Information	Identification
Reg 087	1853/07/03	Tinsley G. Wright	Race: White Sex: Male Age: 7 Months Place of Death: Appomattox Cause of Death: Catarrhal Fever Parent's Names: Wm. P. Wright, Jr. & ___ Where Born: Appomattox Informant: Wm. P. Wright Relation of Informant: Father	1853 Tinsley G. Wright of Appomattox County, son of 1910 William P. Wright of Prince Edward County, grandson of Daniel P. Wright, great grandson of 1811 John Wright of Campbell County, and great great grandson of Robert Wright, Sr. (Campbell County)
Reg 103	1853/12/05	Chs. W. Wright	Race: White Sex: Male Age: 2 Months Place of Death: Appomattox Cause of Death: Hives Parent's Names: W. W. Wright & ____ Where Born: Appomattox Informant: W. W. Wright Relation of Informant: Father	1853 Charles W. Wright of Appomattox County, son of William Washington Wright, grandson of 1881 William P. Wright of Appomattox County, great grandson of Charles Wright, and great great grandson of Robert Wright, Sr. (Campbell County)
Reg 005	1854/09/22	Pryor Wright, Sr.	Race: White Sex: Male Place of Death: Appomattox Cause of Death: Paralysis Where Born: Appomattox Occupation: Farmer Consort of: Marcia Wright Informant: C. S. Wright Relation of Informant: Son	1854 Pryor Rucker Wright, Jr., of Appomattox County, son of 1820 Pryor Wright, Sr., of Prince Edward County and grandson of 1779 John Wright of Prince Edward County

Appendix: Appomattox County, Virginia, Death Records

Book/Page	Date	Decedent	Information	Identification
Reg 020	1855/03/19	Saml. A. Wright	Race: White Sex: Male Age: 78 Place of Death: Appomattox Cause of Death: Paralysis Where Born: Prince Edward Occupation: Farmer Consort of: Barbara G. Informant: Pryor B. Wright Relation of Informant: Son	1854 Samuel A. Wright of Appomattox County, son of 1820 Pryor Wright, Sr., of Prince Edward County and grandson of 1779 John Wright of Prince Edward County
Reg 090	1855/04/22	Sidney Wright	Race: White Sex: Male Age: 6 Days Place of Death: Appomattox Parent's Names: Benj E. & Mary F. Wright Where Born: Appomattox Informant: B.E. Wright Relation of Informant: Father	1855 Sidney Wright of Appomattox County, son of 1880 Benjamin Edward Wright of Amherst County, grandson of 1881 William P. Wright of Appomattox County, great grandson of 1881 Charles Wright, and great great grandson of Robert Wright, Sr. (Campbell County)
Reg 017	1861/01/05	Nancy A. Wright	Race: White Sex: Female Age: 17 Place of Death: Appomattox Cause of Death: Pneumonia Parent's Names: Pryor B. & Lucinda P. Wright Where Born: Prince Edward County Consort of: Unmarried Informant: Pryor B. Wright Relation of Informant: Father	Nancy A. or C. Wright, daughter of 1882 Pryor B. Wright of Appomattox County, granddaughter of 1854 Samuel A. Wright of Appomattox County and granddaughter of 1815 Robert C. Wright of Prince Edward County, great granddaughter of 1820 Pryor Wright, Sr., of Prince Edward County, and great great granddaughter of 1779 John Wright of Prince Edward County

Appendix: Appomattox County, Virginia, Death Records

Book/Page	Date	Decedent	Information	Identification
Reg 049	1862/02/01	Caswell C. Wright	Race: White Sex: Male Age: 26 Place of Death: Mt. Jackson Cause of Death: Typhoid Fever Parent's Names: Pryor B. & Lucinda Wright Where Born: Prince Edward Occupation: Soldier Consort of: Unmarried Informant: Pryor B. Wright Relation of Informant: Father	1862 Caswell C. Wright of Appomattox County, son of 1882 Pryor B. Wright of Appomattox County, grandson of 1854 Samuel A. Wright of Appomattox County and grandson of 1815 Robert C. Wright of Prince Edward County, great grandson of 1820 Pryor Wright, Sr., of Prince Edward County, and great great grandson of 1779 John Wright of Prince Edward County
Reg 027	1864/07/07	Gilliam R. Wright	Race: White Sex: Male Age: 21 Place of Death: Petersburg Cause of Death: Wounds received in battle Parent's Names: Pryor & M. Wright Where Born: Appomattox Consort of: Unmarried Informant: F. C. Wright Relation of Informant: Brother	1864 Gilliam R. Wright of Appomattox County, son of 1854 Pryor Rucker Wright, Jr., of Appomattox County, grandson of 1820 Pryor Wright, Sr., of Prince Edward County, and great grandson of 1779 John Wright of Prince Edward County
Reg 074	1867/07/10	Boyd H. Wright	Race: White Sex: Male Age: 2 Months Place of Death: Appomattox Parent's Names: W. H. & V. Wright Where Born: Appomattox Informant: W. H. Wright Relation of Informant: Father	1867 Boyd H. Wright of Appomattox County, son of W. H. Wright

Appendix: Appomattox County, Virginia, Death Records

Book/Page	Date	Decedent	Information	Identification
Reg 121	1868/02/00	____ Wright	Race: Colored Sex: Female Age: 4 Months Place of Death: Appomattox Parent's Names: Moses & Betsy Wright Where Born: Buckingham Informant: H. E. Gilliam Relation of Informant: Employer	Daughter of Moses Wright
Reg 118	1868/02/11	Phebe Wright	Race: White Sex: Female Age: 100 Place of Death: Appomattox Cause of Death: Old age & suddenly Informant: Dr. D. P. Robertson Relation of Informant: Physician	
Reg 017	1871/04/22	Jillette Wright	Race: White Sex: Female Age: 4 Months Place of Death: Appomattox Cause of Death: Whooping Cough Parent's Names: Wm. W. & Elizabeth Wright Where Born: Appomattox Informant: Wm. W. Wright Relation of Informant: Father	Jillette Wright, daughter of William Washington Wright, granddaughter of 1881 William P. Wright of Appomattox County, great granddaughter of Charles Wright, and great great granddaughter of Robert Wright, Sr. (Campbell County)
Reg 119	1876/06/30	Mildred A. Wright	Race: White Sex: Female Age: 50 Place of Death: Appomattox Cause of Death: Pneumonia Consort of: Camp S. Wright Informant: J. J. D. Relation of Informant: Son	Mildred A. (Martin) (Durriam or Durrum) Wright, wife of Campbell S. Wright, a son of 1854 Pryor Rucker Wright, Jr., of Appomattox County, grandson of 1820 Pryor Wright, Sr., of Prince Edward County, and great grandson of 1779 John Wright of Prince Edward County

Appendix: Appomattox County, Virginia, Death Records

Book/Page	Date	Decedent	Information	Identification
Reg 016	1878/08/00	Erasmus Wright	Race: Colored Sex: Male Age: 5 Months Place of Death: Father's House Parent's Names: Taylor Wright & ____ Where Born: Appomattox Informant: Taylor Wright Relation of Informant: Father	1878 Erasmus Wright of Appomattox County, son of Taylor Wright
Reg 105	1879/09/12	Millie Wright	Race: White Sex: Female Age: 2 Months Place of Death: Appomattox Cause of Death: Inflammation Bowel Parent's Names: W. W. & E. S. Wright Where Born: Appomattox Informant: W. W. Wright Relation of Informant: Father	Millie Wright, daughter of William Washington Wright, granddaughter of 1881 William P. Wright of Appomattox County, great granddaughter of Charles Wright, and great granddaughter of Robert Wright, Sr. (Campbell County)
Reg 069	1880/04/15	York Wright	Race: Colored Sex: Male Age: 55 Place of Death: At his own residence Cause of Death: Cold Where Born: Appomattox County Occupation: Blacksmith Consort of: Gustanna Wright Informant: Gustanna Wright Relation of Informant: Wife	1880 York Wright of Appomattox County

Appendix: Appomattox County, Virginia, Death Records

Book/Page	Date	Decedent	Information	Identification
Reg 079	1881/11/10	____ Wright	Sex: Male Age: 81 Place of Death: Appomattox Cause of Death: Old age Parent's Names: Chas. & Rachel Wright Occupation: Farmer Informant: Wm. W. Wright Relation of Informant: Son	1881 William P. Wright of Appomattox County, son of Charles Wright and grandson of Robert Wright, Sr. (Campbell County)
Reg 088	1882/03/01	Elizabeth S. Wright	Race: White Sex: Female Age: 21 Place of Death: Appomattox County Cause of Death: Consumption Parent's Names: W. W. & Susan F. Wright Where Born: Appomattox County Consort of: Unmarried Informant: W. W. Wright Relation of Informant: Head of Family	Elizabeth S. Wright, daughter of William Wesley Wright
Reg 075	1882/06/08	Prior B. Wright	Race: White Sex: Male Age: 75 Place of Death: Appomattox County Parent's Names: Sam & Barbary Wright Where Born: Appomattox County Occupation: Farmer Consort of: Lucinda P. Wright Relation of Informant: Daughter	1882 Pryor B. Wright of Appomattox County, son of 1854 Samuel A. Wright of Appomattox County, grandson of 1820 Pryor Wright, Sr., of Prince Edward County, and great grandson of 1779 John Wright of Prince Edward County

Appendix: Appomattox County, Virginia, Death Records

Book/Page	Date	Decedent	Information	Identification
Reg 065	1883/04/30	Sam Wright	Race: Colored Sex: Male Age: 26 Place of Death: Father's Residence Cause of Death: Dropsy Parent's Names: Nat and Malinda Wright Where Born: Appomattox County Consort of: Single Name of Informant: Nat Wright Relation of Informant: Head of Family	Sam Wright, son of Nat Wright
Reg 067	1883/07/20	Lizzie J. Wright	Race: Colored Sex: Female Age: 18 Place of Death: Father's Residence Cause of Death: Consumption Parent's Names: York & Gustaanna Wright Where Born: Appomattox County, Virginia Consort of: Single Name of Informant: Gustaanna Wright Relation of Informant: Mother	Lizzie J. Wright, daughter of 1880 York Wright of Appomattox County
Reg 068	1883/08/08	Pomp Wright	Race: Colored Sex: Male Age: 20 Place of Death: Father's Residence Cause of Death: Measles Parent's Names: York & Gustaanna Wright Where Born: Appomattox County Name of Informant: Gustaanna Wright Relation of Informant: Mother	1883 Pomp Wright of Appomattox County, son of 1880 York Wright of Appomattox County

Appendix: Appomattox County, Virginia, Death Records

Book/Page	Date	Decedent	Information	Identification
Reg 122	1886/12/25	Jas. B. Wright	Race: White Sex: Male Age: 8 Months Place of Death: Appomattox County Cause of Death: Teething Parent's Names: Wm. F. & B. W. Wright Where Born: Appomattox County Name of Informant: Wm. F. Wright Relation of Informant: Father	1886 James B. Wright of Appomattox County, son of 1923 William Fletcher Wright of Virginia and grandson of William Wesley Wright
Reg 035	1887/03/25	Maria Wright	Race: Colored Sex: Female Age: 34 Place of Death: Appomattox County	
Reg 130	1888/09/00	Bettie Wright	Race: Colored Sex: Female Age: 15 Place of Death: Appomattox County Parent's Names: J. R. & Jane Wright Consort of: Unmarried Relation of Informant: Family	Bettie Wright, daughter of J. R. Wright
Reg 131	1888/09/00	Fannie Wright	Race: Colored Sex: Female Age: 12 Place of Death: Appomattox County Parent's Names: J. R. & Jane Wright Consort of: Unmarried Relation of Informant: Family	Fannie Wright, daughter of J. R. Wright

Appendix: Appomattox County, Virginia, Death Records

Book/Page	Date	Decedent	Information	Identification
Reg 118	1890/10/01	Gusta Ann Wright	Race: Colored Sex: Female Age: 55 Place of Death: Appomattox County Where Born: Appomattox County, Virginia Name of Informant: Dick Brown Relation of Informant: Son-in-Law	Gusta Anna Wright, widow of 1880 York Wright of Appomattox County
Reg 119	1890/03/01	Minie B. Wright	Race: White Sex: Female Age: 11 Months Place of Death: Appomattox County Cause of Death: Spasm Parent's Names: Jno. W. & Delia Wright Where Born: Appomattox County Consort of: Unmarried Name of Informant: Jno. W. Wright Relation of Informant: Father	Minie B. Wright, daughter of 1914 John W. Wright of Appomattox County and granddaughter of William Wesley Wright
Reg 114	1890/08/01	Martha Wright	Race: White Sex: Female Age: 51 Place of Death: Appomattox County Cause of Death: Tumor Where Born: Appomattox Consort of: Wm. Wright Name of Informant: Wm. Wright Relation of Informant: Husband	Martha (____) Wright, wife of William Wright

Appendix: Appomattox County, Virginia, Death Records

Book/Page	Date	Decedent	Information	Identification
Reg 046	1891/03/00	Harry Wright	Race: Colored Sex: Male Age: 46 Place of Death: Appomattox County Cause of Death: Fever Where Born: Appomattox Occupation: Farmer Name of Informant: Susan Wright Relation of Informant: Wife	
Reg 136	1891/01/00	J. A. Wright	Race: White Sex: Male Age: 20 Place of Death: Appomattox County Cause of Death: Measles Parent's Names: W. W. Wright & _____ Where Born: Appomattox Occupation: Farmer Consort of: Unmarried Name of Informant: W. W. Wright Relation of Informant: Father	1891 James A. Wright of Appomattox County, son of William Wesley Wright
Reg 052	1892/09/00	C. S. Wright	Race: Colored Sex: Male Age: 52 Place of Death: Appomattox County Cause of Death: Stricture Where Born: Apomattox Relation of Informant: Friend	

Book/Page	Date	Decedent	Information	Identification
	1912/09/27	_____ Wright	County: Appomattox	

County: Appomattox
District: Clover Hill
Res in City: 1/2 Day
Sex: female
Race: Negro
Status: single
Born: September 27, 1912
Age: 2 hrs
Occupation:
Birthplace: Appomattox
Father's Name: Ralph Wright
Birthplace: Appomattox
Mother's Name: Martha Misher
Birthplace: Appomattox
Informant:
Filed: Oct 1913
Registrar: F. A. OBrien
Cause: Injuries received during birth
Signed: D. A. Christian Jr M.D.
Address: Veva, Va
Length of Residence:
Burial Place:
Burial Date: Sept 28th 1919
Undertaker: F. A. OBrien

Appendix: Appomattox County, Virginia, Death Records

Book/Page	Date	Decedent	Information	Identification
	1913/01/03	Eliza Wright	County: Appomattox District: Res in City: 48 Yrs Sex: Femail Race: Negro Status: Married Born: unknown, 1865 Age: 48 yrs Occupation: General House Keeping Birthplace: Appomattox Father's Name: Ralph Reed Birthplace: Appomattox Mother's Name: Catherin Reid Birthplace: Appomattox Informant: Chas Elliott Address: Appomattox Va Filed: Registrar: T W. Moses Cause: Heart failure following nervous prostration Contributory: Over work Signed: D. N. Seymour Length of Residence: Place of Burial: Gallilee Cemetery Burial Date: Jany 5, 1912 Undertaker: Thos A Smith Address: Appomattox, Va.	Eliza (Reed) Wright, daughter of Ralph Reed

Appendix: Appomattox County, Virginia, Death Records

Book/Page	Date	Decedent	Information	Identification
	1914/03/10	John W. Wright	County: Appomattox District: South Side Res in City: Sex: Male Race: White Status: Married Born: July 6th Age: 56 yrs Occupation: Mail Carrier Birthplace: Appomattox Father's Name: Wililiam Wright Birthplace: Mother's Name: Mrs. Turner Birthplace: Informant: L. E. Morris Address: Appomattox Filed: Registrar: T W Moses Cause: Apoplexy Contributory: Signed: Jas. B. Abbott Address: Appomattox Va Length of Residence: Place of Burial: Burial Date: Mar 11th, 1914 Undertaker: Miss Emma Smith Address: Appomattox, Va	1914 John W. Wright of Appomattox County, son of William Wesley Wright

Appendix: Appomattox County, Virginia, Death Records

Book/Page	Date	Decedent	Information	Identification
	1914/04/05	Louis Bell Wright	County: Appomattox District: Clover Hill Res in City: Sex: Female Race: White Status: Widowed Born: not known, 1855 Age: 59 yrs Occupation: House wife Birthplace: Appomattox Co Va Father's Name: Joel Ferguson Birthplace: Appomattox Co Va Mother's Name: Roda Conner Birthplace: Appomattox Co Va Informant: John C Ferguson Address: Appomattox Va Filed: May 10, 1914 Registrar: F. A. OBrien Cause: Heart disease Duration: 4 yrs Contributory: Intestinal ____ Duration: 5 yrs Signed: Jas. B Abbott M.D. Date: April 5, 1914 Address: Appomattox Va Place of Burial: Appomattox Burial Date: Apr 6, 1914 Undertaker: Miss Emma Smith Address: Appomatox	Laura Bell (Ferguson) Wright, widow of Christopher W. Wright, a son of Washington Wright

Book/Page	Date	Decedent	Information	Identification
	1916/02/20	Wesley Wright	County: Appomattox District: Southside Res in City: Sex: Male Race: Colored Status: Born: Age: 11 mos Occupation: Birthplace: Appomattox Father's Name: Earnest Wright Birthplace: Appomattox Mother's Name: Narine or Nannie Moseley Birthplace: Appomattox Informant: Ernest Wright Address: Appomattox Filed: 3/19, 1916 Registrar: T. W. Moses Cause: Pneumonia Signed: Dr W. Ferguson Length of Res: Place of Burial: Appomattox Burial Date: Feb 21, 1916 Undertaker: Emma Smith Address: Appomattox	Wesley Wright, son of Earnest Wright

Book/Page	Date	Decedent	Information	Identification
	1918/08/29	Hilda Wright	County: Appomattox District: Clover Hill Res in City: Sex: Female Race: colored Status: single Born: Age: 2 mos Occupation: Birthplace: Appomattox Father's Name: Yoles Wright Birthplace: Appomattox Mother's Name: Mary Moseley Birthplace: Appomattox Informant: Mary Moseley Address: Appomattox Filed: Jan 7, 1919 Registrar: T. W. O'Brien Cause: No Dr. Length of Res: Place of Burial: Appomattox Burial Date: Aug 30th, 1918 Undertaker: T. A. Smith Address: Appomattox	

Book/Page	Date	Decedent	Information	Identification
	1918/09/01	Blanche Walker Wright	County: Appomattox District: Clover Hill Res in City: Sex: Female Race: White Status: Married Born: Age: 56 yrs Occupation: Housewife Birthplace: Campbell Co. Father's Name: Jim Law Birthplace: Buckingham Mother's Name: Betty Drickard Birthplace: Campbell Informant: W. F. Wright Address: Appomattox Filed: Jun 7, 1917 Registrar: F. W. O'Brien Cause: T.B. of bowels Contributory: T. B. Peritonitis Signed: D. N. Tuppman M.D. Address: Appomattox Va Length of Res: Place of Burial: Appomattox Burial Date: Sept 2, 1918 Undertaker: T. A. Smith &c Address: Appomattox Va	Blanche Walker (Lane) Wright, wife of 1923 William Fletcher Wright of Appomattox County, a son of William Wesley Wright

Book/Page	Date	Decedent	Information	Identification
	1918/11/27	Lucy Emeline Wright	County: Appomattox District: Cloverhill Res in City: Sex: feminine Race: White Status: Born: November 11, 1914 Age: 4 yrs Occupation: Birthplace: Virginia Father's Name: G. W. Wright Birthplace: Virginia Mother's Name: Fannie Banton Birthplace: Virginia Informant: Filed: March 10, 1918 Registrar: F. A. OBrien Cause: Pneumonia Bronchitis followed influenza Signed: D. N. Tupman Address: Appomattox Length of Res: Place of Burial: Burial Date: Nov 28, 1918 Undertaker: Evergreen Supply Co Address: Appomattox	

Appendix: Appomattox County, Virginia, Death Records

Book/Page	Date	Decedent	Information	Identification
	1920/06/15	Jane Wright	County: Appomattox District: Clover Hill Length of Res: Sex: Female Race: Colored Status: Married Born: Age: 80 yrs Occupation: Housewife Birthplace: Appomattox Co. Father's Name: Richard Anderson Birthplace: Appomattox Mother's Name: Lucinda not known Birthplace: not known Informant: Tom Kelso Address: Vera Va Filed: Dec 10, 1920 Registrar: F. A. O'Brien Cause: not seen in last illness Place of Burial: Appomattox Burial Date: June 18th 1920 Undertaker: S. G. Scott & Co Address: Appomattox	

Book/Page	Date	Decedent	Information	Identification
	1920/08/09	Mary Anne Wright	County: Appomattox District: Stonewall Sex: Female Race: Colored Status: Marrid Spouse: Luther Wright Born: Age: 52 years Occupation: Housewife Birthplace: Appomattox Co Father's Name: London Mosley Birthplace: Appomattox Co Mother's Name: Lincinda Wood Birthplace: Campbell Co Informant: Walker Mosley Address: Concord Depot Va Filed: Aug 9, 1920 Registrar: W C Turner Cause: Paralysis Duration: 1 yr Autopsy? No Signed: R N Cran Date: Aug 9th 1920 Address: Concord Depot Va Place of Burial: Spent Spring Va Burial Date: Aug 10th 1920 Undertaker: Address:	

Book/Page	Date	Decedent	Information	Identification
	1920/12/03	Jim Wright	County: Appomattox District: Clover Hill Sex: Male Race: Colored Status: Widowed Spouse: Born: Age: 84 years Occupation: Farmer Birthplace: Buckingham Father's Name: Dick Wright Birthplace: Buckingham Mother's Name: not known Birthplace: not known Informant: William Wright Address: Vera Va Registrar: F A OBrien Cause: No Dr. Suppose Old Age Place of Burial: Appomattox Burial Date: Dec 4, 1920 Undertaker: L. A. Smith & Co Address: Appomattox	

INDEX

WRIGHT FAMILY

PROBATE RECORDS

APPOMATTOX COUNTY, VIRGINIA

1845 to 1900

Revised as of November 3, 2005

Introduction To Appendix: Probate Records for Appomattox County, Virginia

This document is an appendix to a larger work titled Sorting Some Of The Wrights Of Southern Virginia. The work is divided into parts for each family of Wrights that has been researched. Each part is divided into two sections; the first section is text discussing the family and the evidence supporting the relationships and the second section is a descendants chart summarizing the relationships and information known about each individual.

The appendices to the work (of which this document is one) present source records for persons named Wright by county and by type of record with the identification of the person named and their Wright ancestors to the extent known.

The source for the records listed in this appendix is the following:

1) Appomattox County, Virginia, Probate Records, available from the Clerk of the Circuit Court, P.O. Box 672, Appomattox, Virginia 24522.

The identification of a person or their ancestor by year and county indicates their year of death and county of residence at death. For example, "1763 Thomas Wright of Bedford County" indicates that this was the Thomas Wright who died in 1763 in Bedford County. If no state is listed after the county, the state is Virginia; counties in states other than Virginia will have a state listed after the county, as in "1876 William S. Wright of Highland County, Ohio".

A parenthetical after the name indicates an identification of the person when a place of death is not yet known, as in "John Wright (Goochland County Carpenter)". A county in parentheses after the name indicates the county with which that person was most identified when no evidence of the place of death has yet been found, as in "Grief Wright (Bedford County)".

All or portions of the text and descendants charts for each Wright family identified are available from the author:

Robert N. Grant
15 Campo Bello Court   (H) 650-854-0895
Menlo Park, California 94025 (O) 650-614-3800

This is a work in progress and I would be most interested in receiving additional information about any of the persons identified in these records in order to correct any errors or expand on the information given.

Appendix: Appomattox County, Virginia, Probate Records

Book/Page	Date	Decedent	Document	Identification

Records before 1892 were burned

No Wrights listed

Other Heritage Books by Robert N. Grant

Identifying the Wrights in the Goochland County, Virginia Tithe Lists, 1732-84

The Identification of 1809 William Wright of Franklin County, Virginia, as the Son of 1792 John Wright of Fauquier County, Virginia, and Elizabeth (Bronaugh) (Darnall) Wright

Wright Family Birth Records (1853-1896) and Marriage Records (1788-1915): Franklin County, Virginia, 1853-1896

Wright Family Birth Records (1853-1896) and Marriage Records (1782-1900): Campbell County, Virginia

Wright Family Birth Records, Marriage Records, and Personal Property Tax Lists: Appomattox County, Virginia

Wright Family Census Records, Deed Records, Land Tax Lists, Death Records and Probate Records: Appomattox County, Virginia

Wright Family Census Records: Bedford County, Virginia, 1810-1900

Wright Family Census Records: Campbell County, Virginia, 1810-1900

Wright Family Census Records: Franklin County, Virginia, 1810-1900

Wright Family Death Records (1853-1920), Cemetery Records by Cemetery, and Probate Records (1782-1900): Campbell County, Virginia

Wright Family Death Records (1854-1920), Cemetery Records by Cemetery, and Probate Records (1785-1928): Franklin County, Virginia

Wright Family Death, Cemetery and Probate Records: Bedford County, Virginia

Wright Family Deed Records (1782-1900) and Land Tax List (1782-1850): Campbell County, Virginia

Wright Family Land Grants (1785-1900) and Deed Records (1785-1897): Franklin County, Virginia

Wright Family Land Grants, Deed Records, Land Tax List, Death Records, Probate Records: Prince Edward County, Virginia

Wright Family Land Records: Bedford County, Virginia

Wright Family Land Tax Lists: Franklin County, Virginia, 1786-1860

Wright Family Personal Property Tax Lists: Campbell County, Virginia, 1785-1850

Wright Family Personal Property Tax Lists: Franklin County, Virginia, 1786-1850

Wright Family Personal Property Tax Records for Bedford County, Virginia, 1782 to 1850

Wright Family Records: Births in Bedford County, Virginia

Wright Family Records: Land Tax List, Bedford County, Virginia, 1782-1850

Wright Family Records: Lynchburg, Virginia Birth Records (1853-1896), Marriage Records (1805-1900), Marriage Notices (1794-1880), Census Records (1900), Deed Records (1805-1900), Death Records (1853-1896), Probate Records (1805-1900)

Wright Family Records: Marriages in Bedford County, Virginia

Wright Family Records: Prince Edward County, Virginia Birth Records, Marriage Records, Election Polls, and Tithe List, Personal Property Tax List, Census